INSIGHTS 2021

Junko Murao
Akiko Miyama
Tomoko Tsujimoto
Kana Yokoyama
Ashley Moore

KINSEIDO

Kinseido Publishing Co., Ltd.
3-21 Kanda Jimbo-cho, Chiyoda-ku,
Tokyo 101-0051, Japan

First published 2021 by Kinseido Publishing Co., Ltd.

はじめに

このテキストは、文化・環境・技術・社会・教育・医療・科学・ビジネス・ファッションといった幅広い分野の記事を取り上げています。全世界で起きた前例のない新型コロナウイルスによるパンデミック以後、世界は大きく変化しつつあります。このテキストでは、生きた英語を学び、広い視野を養えるよう国内外の様々なトピックの記事を選んでおります。各章の話題は、新型コロナウイルス感染症拡大以後の世界は、新型コロナウイルス感染症拡大以前の世界からどのように変化していくのかといったような観点から、ディスカッションしていただくトピックとしてもご利用いただけます。本テキストを授業内での様々な活動にお役立て頂ければと思います。

●Key Expressions 1

写真などの視覚情報を見てトピックへの関心を促す、リーディング・セクション読解のためのキーワードのブランク埋めの問題です。キーワードを耳で聞くだけでなく、最初の一文字と語数をヒントにして、辞書も参照しながら解答してみてください。リーディング・セクションの背景知識を構築しながら、辞書を用いて文法も確認する練習問題となっています。

●Key Expressions 2

リーディング・セクション中に登場する重要表現や、TOEIC にも出現頻度の高い語彙を学習するエクササイズです。単なるキーワードの意味理解だけでなく、関連語句や派生語を構成する接頭辞・接尾辞の意味など、単語力増強に必要な情報が盛り込まれています。

●Key Expressions 3

話題に関連した構文や語法の練習問題です。基礎的な文法力も試せる問題となっています。

●Background Knowledge

リーディング・セクションの背景を構築する短い記事を読み、簡単な速読用の設問を解きます。一語一句訳すのではなく、必要な情報のみを拾い読みするという速読方法（スキャニング）で読んでみて下さい。語彙の類推力を養うために、問題解答に関係するところには、あえて注は付けておりませんので、辞書を参照せずに解答してみましょう。

●Newspaper English

文法確認のセクションです。ただし、網羅的に文法を扱ってはいません。英文記事を読むために最低限必要な文法の基礎知識や表現ルールを学びます。

●Reading

本セクションを読むまでに、かなりの背景知識・文法・語彙の構築ができています。ここまでのセクションをしっかり復習しておけば、辞書なしでもほぼ理解できるでしょう。読解の助けになる注は付けていますが、できるだけ注を参照しないで読むよう心がけてください。

●Summary, Comprehension 1&2

リーディング・セクションの内容が理解できているかどうかのチェックを行います。

以上のようなヴァラエティに富んだ練習問題によって、英字新聞やインターネットのニュース記事を抵抗感なく読めるようになるはずです。最後になりましたが、テキスト作成の際にお世話になりました金星堂編集部の皆様に心からお礼を申し上げます。

編著者

● 英字新聞を知ろう ●

英字新聞を目の前にすると、一体どこからどのように読んでいけばよいのか迷う方もおられるでしょう。まずは、以下のジャパンタイムズ紙のフロントページ（第一面）やジャパンニューズ紙のオンライン版トップページを見ながら、英字新聞を読む際に知っておくべきことを学びましょう。大きなニュースは繰り返しフロントページで取り上げられることがあります。まずはこのページで、持続性があり、興味を持てる話題を選択し、しばらくそのニュースを追いかけていく読み方がお勧めです。同じ話題のニュースに何度も触れていると、次第に辞書なしで読めるようになるでしょう。

1．紙媒体のフロントページの構成

新聞社のロゴ（Logo）

これは紙媒体のジャパンタイムズ紙のフロントページです。ジャパンタイムズ紙は、ニューヨークタイムズ紙とセットで発行されており、国内・海外の情報を幅広く提供しています。

124TH YEAR | NO. 43,069

www.japantimes.co.jp

ALL THE NEWS WITHOUT FEAR OR FAVOR

the japan times

INCORPORATING The New York Times INTERNATIONAL EDITION

IN TODAY'S NYT: ITALY FIGHTS WAR AGAINST CORONAVIRUS ON TWO FRONTS PAGE 1

BUSINESS: OPPORTUNITY COMES CALLING Firms see boost from increased online meetings | PAGE 3

INSIGHTS: A QUESTION OF CULTURE Are Japan's social norms limiting infections? | PAGE 4

FRIDAY, APRIL 24, 2020 ¥230

Current approach creates lack of clarity: experts

Limited virus testing casts doubt on data

KYODO

The lower the positive rate with more tests conducted, the better.

Resetting the political calendar after COVID-19

Commentary

MICHAEL MACARTHUR BOSACK PYEONGTAEK, SOUTH KOREA

2020 was set to be a highlight year for many Japanese politicians, but the disruptions from COVID-19 have affected the political calendar in important ways.

BOJ eyes new round of stimulus

Central bank could expand purchases of commercial bonds

Pachinko parlors show limits of shutdown

BLOOMBERG

「グローバル人材の採用」ならロバート・ウォルターズ

ROBERT WALTERS

INSIDE TODAY

NATIONAL	2	TV/WEATHER	10
BUSINESS	3	SPOTLIGHT	11, 12
INSIGHTS	4		
WORLD	5-7		
SPORTS	8		
OPINION	9		

Earth becomes wilder, cleaner

Coronavirus outbreak updates

jtimes.jp/covid19

HOTEL CYCLE

The Japan Times PAGE: 1

重要記事の紹介

各紙面から大きなニュースを取り上げ簡単に紹介しています。

ヘッドライン（Headline）

ヘッドラインの詳しい説明はp.6参照。

リード（Lead）

記事の書き出しの一段落目のことをリードと呼びます。ニュースの概略が紹介されます。リードには、5W1Hの情報ができるだけ盛り込まれます。

キャプション（Caption）

図版や写真につく説明文のことです。記事を読むときの大切な背景知識を提供しています。先に目を通しておくと記事の理解の助けとなります。

目次

記事のジャンルと掲載ページが提示されます。

2．オンライン版のトップページ

新聞社のロゴ（Logo）

これは読売新聞の英語版ジャパンニューズ紙のトップページです。紙媒体とは異なり、文字数を減らし、視覚情報の多い作りとなっています。ヘッドラインをクリックすると記事全体が読めます。

The Japan News by The Yomiuri Shimbun

NEWS BLOG 読売新聞(Japanese Edition) Login SignUp

TOP | POLITICS | SOCIETY | BUSINESS | WORLD | SPORTS | EDITORIAL | FEATURES | COLUMNS | POP&CULTURE | ALL GENRES

SUBSCRIBE NEWSPAPER

Japan set to allow more coronavirus patients to recuperate at home PREMIUM

As national population declines, Tokyo sees overconcentration PREMIUM

The population of Japan logged a record drop of more than 500,000 in one year, the highest number since the first such survey was conducted in 1968 and the 11th straight year of decline since its peak in 2009, according to a government report. The report also revealed that the population is concentr...

Image Index

Olympic rings towed away from Tokyo Bay, for... PREMIUM

Hiroshima mayor calls for unity against nucl... PREMIUM

Japan apparel makers to tighten straps to su... PREMIUM

Coronavirus in Japan

Concerned about the virus?

More News & Features

Olympic rings towed away from Tokyo Bay, for now PREMIUM

Hiroshima mayor calls for unity against nuclear weapons, novel coronavirus PREMIUM

HIROSHIMA — Hiroshima Mayor Kazumi Matsui on Thursday called for unity in the battle against nuclear weapons and the novel coronavirus at a memorial ceremony to commemorate the 75th anniversary of t...

Japan apparel makers to tighten straps to survive amid pandemic PREMIUM

Japan orchestrating 1st joint cyber drill with U.S., key nations PREMIUM

Japan is finalizing a plan to conduct a joint exercise with nations including the United States aimed at combatting cyber-attacks as soon as this autumn, The Yomiuri Shimbun has learned. This would...

Tokyo confirms 360 virus cases

Three hundred and sixty novel coronavirus infection cases were newly confirmed on Thursday, it has been learned. The number of people infected per day passed 300 for the first time since Tuesday, and ...

Health ministry refutes Osaka gov.'s plug for gargle treatment of virus PREMIUM

Hiroshima photographer strives to pass down experience of hibakusha through family photos PREMIUM

Seventy-five years have passed since the atomic bombings of Hiroshima and Nagasaki. With the average age of hibakusha, or surviving atomic bombing victims, surpassing 83, questions have been raised o...

Japan prime minister: Measures against coronavirus are top priority now PREMIUM

Now is not the time to dissolve the House of Representatives and hold a general election, Prime Minister Shinzo Abe said in a recent interview with the monthly magazine Chuokoron. "If there is a n...

Japan soccer star Miura rewrites another age-related record, plays in league cup match at 53 PREMIUM

Deepen discussions on challenges of realizing central bank digital currency PREMIUM

Research on the issuance of digital currency by central banks is progressing around the world. The Bank of Japan has set up a new department to deal with the issue and started full-fledged discussi...

Japan's Foreign Minister to visit Southeast Asian countries PREMIUM

Japan News Digital Membership

Food

Travel

Voices from Japan

Asia News

Culture & Lifestyle

Experiencing Japan

Manga & Anime

Japan News Weekly ePaper

Troubleshooter

Reviews

Gift Suggestions

Language Learning

History at your fingertips

A unique archive, all the way back to 1874 The Yomiuri Shimbun and The Japan News

Opinion & Analysis

Comic Strip: Neko Pitcher

Tokyo 2020

TSUMUGU Project

Weather

Tokyo 09:00 pm

28.4°C

Sat Sun Mon Tue

Market Data

Exchange Rates

¥/$ 104.61 - 106.61

¥/€ 123.18 - 126.18

Topix Close

1549.88 -4.83

記事のカテゴリー

各項目をクリックすると、政治・社会・ビジネス・スポーツなど、カテゴリー別に記事を日をさかのぼって読むことができます。

トップニュース

（Top News）

紙媒体のフロントページに載る重要記事が紹介されます。

その他の重要記事や特集の紹介

3. ヘッドラインの特徴

ヘッドラインの英文はいくつかのルールに則って書かれています。文字数を少なくし、簡潔に表現するための工夫がなされます。以下のもっともよく使用されるルールを上げておきましたので参考にしてください。

① 記事を新鮮に見せるために動詞を現在形にする。過去・現在完了は現在形で表す。
Government renews call for self-isolation「政府再び自粛要請」（*The Japan Times*, April 23, 2020）

②「進行形・近接未来」や「受動態」では be 動詞が省略され、それぞれ、V-ing や V-ed の形で表される。
North Korea facing food shortages「北朝鮮が食糧不足に直面している」
309 cases confirmed in Tokyo「東京で 309 名のコロナウイルス感染が確認された」

③ 未来は不定詞（to V）で表されることが多い。
Japanese govt to extend period for subsidies「日本政府、助成金支払い期間を延長」

④ 冠詞や be 動詞は省略されることが多い。
Banks still busy despite pandemic「パンデミックにも関わらず銀行なおも繁忙」
Fossilized dinosaur egg found in Japan recognized as world's smallest
「日本で発見された恐竜の卵の化石、世界最小と認められる」（*The Japan Times*, April 5, 2020）

⑤ say(s) の代わりにコロン(:)を用いることがある。
Distancing needed into 2022: study
「社会的距離の必要 2022 年まで、とある調査」（*The Japan Times*, April 19, 2020）

⑥ 省略や略語が多用される。
tech → technology（技術）　Govt → Government（政府）
uni prof. → university professor（大学教授）
HK → Hong Kong（香港）　BOJ → The Bank of Japan（日本銀行）
VW → Volkswagen　（フォルクスワーゲン）

⑦ カンマによって and が省略される。
Earth becomes wilder, cleaner during lockdowns「ロックダウン中、地球はより野性的でクリーンに」

⑧ 短い綴りの語が好まれる。
vie「張り合う、競争する」　eye「目をつける」　nix「拒否する、禁止する」
ink「署名する」　near「近づく」

4. 英字新聞攻略法

さて、新聞全体の構成がわかったところで、どのように英字新聞に親しんでいけばいいのでしょうか。

① 英字新聞の言語的特徴に慣れよう
英字新聞は、ニュースを新鮮に見せるために**3. ヘッドラインの特徴**で見たように、ヘッドラインを現在形で書くなど、読者を引きつける様々な工夫がなされています。本書では、その工夫に関して **Newspaper English** のセクションで取り上げていますので、問題を解答しながら、まずその特徴を覚えましょう。

② すべての記事を読む必要はない
すべての記事を隅々まで読むのは大変ですし、その必要もありません。まずは、ヘッドラインや写真などを見て、興味のある記事だけを読んでみましょう。英字新聞に慣れるまでは、できるだけ日本に関する記事を選ぶほうが読みやすいでしょう。

③ リード・写真・キャプションは背景知識を提供するものなので、最初に目を通そう
記事の本文は、リードに最重要情報が置かれ、パラグラフが進むにつれ情報の重要度が下がってきますから、しばらくはリードだけに挑戦するのもよいでしょう。

④ 特定のテーマに絞って読むようにしよう

特定のテーマを継続して読む方法が英語学習には最適です。あるテーマに特有の語彙をまとめて学習することができるので、類似テーマの記事なら簡単に読めるようになるからです。

Insights 2021 Table of Contents

Chapter 1

Accepting Diversity

おもてなし最前線

UNIX

● Key Expressions 1

CD1-02

音声を聞いて１～３の（　　）内に適当な語を書き入れましょう。

1. A Muslim woman talks with a (f _ _ _ _ _) hairdresser at UNIX's Omiya outlet in Saitama.
埼玉にあるUNIX直営の大宮店で、イスラム教徒の女性が女性美容師と話している。

2. Some Muslims believe that women should (r _ _ _ _ _ _) from showing their hair in front of men.
女性が男性の前で髪を見せることを控えるべきと思っているイスラム教徒もいる。

3. The Muslimah Beauty service is (a _ _ _ _ _ _ _ _) at a Tokyo-based beauty salon where female customers can have their hair cut without worrying about being seen by men.
ムスリマ（女性イスラム教徒）ビューティーサービスは、東京に拠点を置く美容室で利用でき、そこでは女性客は男性に見られることを心配せずに髪を切ってもらえる。

● Key Expressions 2

記事に登場する人物の感情や感覚を説明するためにa sense of...（～感／感覚）という表現が使われることがあります。

以下の１～５の日本語に該当する表現になるように、選択肢から適当な語句を選び、（　　）内に書き入れましょう。

1. 安心感を与える　(　　　　　　　　) a sense of (　　　　　　　　)
2. 達成感を感じる　(　　　　　　　　) a sense of (　　　　　　　　)
3. 疎外感に苦しむ　(　　　　　　　　) a sense of (　　　　　　　　)
4. 期待感を抱く　(　　　　　　　　) a sense of (　　　　　　　　)
5. 方向感覚を失う　(　　　　　　　　) one's sense of (　　　　　　　　)

最初の空所に入る語句

suffer from	offer	feel	lose	have

2番目の空所に入る語

accomplishment	expectation	alienation	relief	direction

● Key Expressions 3

不定詞の「意味上の主語」が文の主語と異なるときは、不定詞の直前に明記します。日本語訳を参考に、以下の１～４の英文の[　　]内の語句を正しい語順に並べかえましょう。なお、文頭に来る語も小文字で与えられています。

1. [for / no suitable places / to / there were / pray / her] in the hair salon.
その美容室内には、彼女が祈るのに適当な場所がなかった。

____

2. [difficult / her / it / for / is / to find] salons that she can visit.
彼女が訪れることができるサロンを見つけるのは難しい。

____

3. She [want / not / does / a male hairdresser / her hair / cut / to].
彼女は男性美容師に自分の髪の毛をカットしてもらいたくない。

____

4. Offering amenities at the hair salon is a good idea [to / for / safe / feel / Muslim women].
その美容室で快適な備品を提供することは、イスラム教徒の女性が安心するのによいアイディアである。

____

● Background Knowledge

美容室 UNIX の岡本尚樹営業本部長のコメントの内容について、英文に述べられているものを 1 ～ 4 から選びましょう。

"The skills of Japanese hairdressers have won high praise from East Asian women, whose hair has characteristics similar to that of Japanese women," said Naoki Okamoto, head of the company's sales promotion department. "I would like Muslimah customers to experience the exceptional techniques of our stylists," said Okamoto, who is also a hairdresser.

The Asahi Shimbun

1. 日本人美容師のスキルは世界中から称賛されている。
2. 東アジアの女性と日本人女性の髪質は同じような特徴がない。
3. 東アジアの女性は日本人美容師のテクニックを高く評価している。
4. 特にイスラム教徒の客に、同美容室のスタイリストのテクニックを宣伝してもらいたい。

● Newspaper English

新聞記事では、ある行為を他人に「行ってもらう」ことを表す使役構文が使われていることがあります。代表的な使役動詞 have を使った「have+ 行為者 + 動詞の原形」や「have+ 行為を受ける対象 + 動詞の過去分詞形」の表現を覚えておきましょう。

以下の 1 と 2 の（　　）内に当てはまる語を選択肢から選び、書き入れましょう。

1. A student from Indonesia previously had her hair (　　　　　　　) only after returning to her home country.

2. She always has a female hairdresser (　　　　　　　) her hair.

treat	treated

Reading

Saitama beauty salon allows Muslimahs to let their hair down

SAITAMA—Privacy, prayer mats and alcohol-free shampoo are among the amenities at a hair salon in Japan catering to Muslim women, many of whose faith restricts them from showing their hair in front of men.

The Muslimah Beauty service is available at the Omiya outlet of Tokyo-based beauty salon operator UNIX.

As women of Muslim faith can remove their hijab scarves in a dedicated private area separated by curtains to discuss hairstyle and color with a female hairdresser, they can have their hair cut and dyed without worrying about being seen by men.

Shampoo and hair treatment without alcohol are used in accordance with Islamic laws, and a special mat for praying is also available.

Dhyah, 24, a student from Indonesia who has lived in Japan for six years and uses the hair salon, said she previously had her hair treated only after returning to her home country, as there were no suitable places for her to have it cut in Japan.

“The service is very nice, as it offers a sense of relief,” she said. “I’d like to recommend it to friends.”

The Muslimah haircut service started being offered on a full-scale basis at the outlet in May, with prices starting from 7,000 yen ($66) for a haircut. Few beauty salons provide such services in Saitama Prefecture, according to UNIX officials.

UNIX decided to introduce the service after a meeting of tenants at a commercial complex in Chiba that houses one of its outlets.

Naoki Okamoto, 43, head of the company’s sales promotion department, became interested in a campaign to attract Islamic customers at the gathering. He learned that Muslimahs were struggling in this country to find salons that

- prayer mat「礼拝用の敷物」
- cater to...「～用の、～に対応する」
- hijab「ヒジャブ（イスラム教徒の女性が頭や体を覆う布）」
- dedicated「専用の」
- in accordance with...「～に従って」
- previously「以前は」
- on a full-scale basis「本格的に」
- official「関係者」
- commercial complex「商業施設」
- house...「～を入れる、～を収容する」
- struggle「苦労する」

they could visit without anxiety and proposed the new service after studying Islamic practices.

The Muslimah haircut service was introduced at the Chiba outlet in November 2016. As it proved to be popular, the service was also adopted in the Omiya shop in Saitama Prefecture, where UNIX was founded.

The Asahi Shimbun

anxiety「不安、心配」
propose...「～を提案する」
practice「慣習」
prove to be...「～だとわかる」
adopt...「～を採用する」

● Summary

CD1-05

以下の空所１～４に当てはまる語を選択肢から選び、書き入れましょう。

A Japanese beauty salon (1.) has introduced a service catering to Muslim women who choose to cover their (2.) in public. The new (3.) includes alcohol-free products, prayer facilities, a female stylist and a private (4.) where they can receive treatments and haircuts away from the gaze of men.

service	operator	area	hair

● Comprehension 1

UNIX 直営の大宮店のムスリマビューティーサービスで提供されていないものを 1 ～ 4 から選びましょう。

1. Alcohol-free spaces
2. Special mats for praying
3. Exclusive areas for Muslimah clients
4. Female staff serving Muslimahs

● Comprehension 2

本文の内容に合うように、1 と 3 の英文を完成させるのに適当なものを、2 の質問の答えとして適当なものを、a ～ d から選びましょう。

1. The Omiya branch of UNIX
a. is only staffed by other women.
b. offers a space that is comfortable for Muslim women.
c. does not accept male customers.
d. has Muslim hair stylists on its staff.

2. Before finding the salon, when did the Indonesian student have her hair treated?
a. During visits back to her home country
b. When Muslim friends visited her apartment
c. On special trips she made to Chiba
d. Whenever family and friends came to see her in Japan

3. The company was inspired to begin offering the service after
a. some customers complained about the use of products containing alcohol.
b. the head of its sales promotion department converted to Islam.
c. struggling to attract new customers in a shrinking market.
d. hearing about difficulties local Muslim women encountered.

Chapter 2

Washi Helps Us Get Through Summer

和紙の底力

SASAWASHI Co.,Ltd. (left) / Hosokawa-Tex, Inc. (right)

● Key Expressions 1

CD1-06

写真に関する音声を聞いて１～３の（　　）内に適当な語を書き入れましょう。

1. The hat and the pair of shoes are made with (t _ _ _ _ _ _ _ _ _ _) Japanese "washi" paper.
   （上の写真に写っている）帽子と一足の靴は伝統的な和紙で作られている。

2. They are (c _ _ _ _ _ _ _) on at home and abroad, opening up a new wave of interest in the washi paper.
   それらは国内外で人気を集めており、和紙に対する新たな関心の波が寄せられている。

3. The products are (c _ _ _ _ _ _ _ _ _ _ _ _) by being light in weight and highly moisture absorbent.
   それらの製品は軽量で、吸湿性が高いのが特徴である。

● Key Expressions 2

企業の製品を取材した記事では、「〜できる」という意味を持つ語尾が -able で終わる形容詞を用いて、その製品の機能（function）が紹介されることがあります。

枠内の接尾辞の説明を参考に、以下の１〜５の日本語に該当する形容詞になるように、選択肢から適当な語を選び、書きかえましょう。

1. 洗うことができる　(　　　　　　　　　　)
2. 快適な　(　　　　　　　　　　)
3. 耐久性のある　(　　　　　　　　　　)
4. 身に着けることができる　(　　　　　　　　　　)
5. 通気性のある　(　　　　　　　　　　)

breathe	dure	wear	wash	comfort

● Key Expressions 3

以下の１〜４は、ある和紙を使った靴の製品の特長（feature）を説明しています。日本語訳を参考に［　　］内の語句を正しい語順に並べかえましょう。なお、文頭に来る語も小文字で与えられています。

1. The [easily worn / can / shoes / be].
その靴は履きやすい。

2. The fabric used for the shoes is [stronger / seven / nearly / times] in abrasion resistance than canvas cloth.
その靴に使用される生地は、耐摩耗性がキャンバス布の 7 倍近くである。

3. The surface of the shoes that comes in contact with the skin is 100 percent washi paper, [is / breathable / which / highly] and moisture absorbent.
肌と接触する靴の表面は、通気性と吸湿性が高い 100%の和紙である。

4. [only about / each / weighs / shoe] 140 grams, around half the weight of a regular slip-on shoe made with canvas cloth.
靴の片方の重量はわずか 140 グラムほどで、キャンバス布で作られた通常のスリッポンの靴の約半分の重量である。

● Background Knowledge

自然素材の「くまざさ」を原料とした和紙を使った製品を製造販売しているSASAWASHI株式会社について、英文に述べられていないものを1～4から選びましょう。

SASAWASHI Co. has been handling assorted goods made of washi paper thread for more than 10 years, with over 100 stores nationwide carrying its products. The company's sales have grown to about 200 million yen ($1.88 million) a year. Its socks and slippers, boasting a smooth feel, have prompted increased inquiries from the United States, European countries and South Korea.

"We want to promote sales in overseas markets in a proactive manner," a director of the company said.

The Asahi Shimbun

1. 10年以上にわたって和紙で作られた糸を使った商品を販売してきた。
2. 全国100軒を超える店舗で商品を販売している。
3. 販売高は、年間およそ2億円である。
4. 取締役は、これから海外市場向けの商品開発を開始したいと思っている。

● Newspaper English

新聞記事のヘッドライン（見出し）では、切れ味のよい表現にするために、be動詞や冠詞がしばしば省略されます。また、見出しの最後にはピリオドは付きません。

以下の1～3の（　　）内に当てはまる適当な語を選択肢から選び、適当な形に変化させてヘッドラインを完成させましょう。

1. Japanese washi paper (　　　　　　　　) its way both at home and abroad
和紙が国内外に進出している

2. Moisture-killing washi (　　　　　　　　) brave new forms
湿気を防ぐ和紙が挑戦的な新しい形をとろうとしている

3. Osaka-based company: Washi functions (　　　　　　　　) even after being washed
大阪府を本拠地とする会社によると、和紙の機能は洗った後でさえ保持されている

retain	take	make

Reading

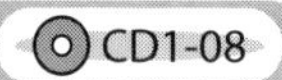

Paper shoes? Moisture-killing washi taking brave new forms

Hats, arm covers and even shoes made from traditional Japanese "washi" paper are catching on at home and abroad, opening up a new wave of interest in the durable material.

The products are not only light, but also protect the skin from ultraviolet rays and prevent stickiness from sweat, making them an ideal choice for getting through hot summer days.

"We want to promote the merits of the traditional material," said Toshinori Itoi, a director at SASAWASHI Co., which designs, manufactures and sells soft goods in Izumiotsu, Osaka Prefecture.

The products are made of yarn that is formed by twisting together thin, tape-like strips of washi. Since they are made of paper, the products are light in weight and highly moisture absorbent, in addition to filtering out 90 percent of UV rays. The company also added antibacterial and deodorant functions by blending flakes of "kumazasa" bamboo grass into the washi.

Hats and arm covers are among the most popular products, Itoi said. There has been an increasing number of days of intense sunshine and heat during the summer in Japan in recent years, and the paper-based fashion accessories have become popular mainly among women who say the products help maintain the skin's smooth feel.

"A growing number of purchases are made by people who suffer from sensitive skin or allergies," Itoi said.

The washi paper is also appealing because its functions, which come from the material itself, are retained even after being washed.

Hosokawa-Tex, Inc., a long-established textile company based in Kamiichi, Toyama Prefecture, produced shoes made with washi paper for the first time in Japan. With the help of

stickiness「べたつき」
get through...「～を過ごす」
promote...「～を売り込む」
soft goods「織物製品」
yarn「織り糸」
strip「細長い一片」
filter out...「～を防ぐ」
antibacterial「抗菌の」
deodorant「防臭の」
flake「薄片」
intense「強烈な」
maintain...「～を維持する」
purchase「購入」
sensitive「敏感な」
allergy「アレルギー」
come from...「～に由来する」
long-established「老舗の」
textile「繊維の」

a shoe manufacturer in Kobe, the company went through many prototypes before launching its first product in April last year. The washi shoes caused a stir after about 4,000 pairs were sold mainly through the company's online shop. They are made with a fabric intertwined with a washi paper thread made from Manila hemp.

"We have an increasing number of repeat customers, and people appreciate the charm of the product," said Managing Director Kotaro Hosokawa. "We want to market it as a material to shoe manufacturers at home and abroad."

The Asahi Shimbun

prototype「試作品」
launch...「～を発売する」
cause a stir「評判となる」
intertwine...「～を織り込む」
appreciate...「～を評価する」

Summary

以下の空所１～４に当てはまる語を選択肢から選び、書き入れましょう。

Clothing items (1.   ) from traditional Japanese "washi" paper are proving to be popular with customers both in Japan and overseas. The appeal of washi as a clothing fabric is (2.   ) by its relatively light weight, moisture absorbency, and ability to offer some protection from ultraviolet rays. These characteristics, (3.   ) even after being (4.   ), make washi-based clothing particularly attractive during hotter summer months.

washed	enhanced	retained	made

● Comprehension 1

SASAWASHI 株式会社について本文で述べられているものを 1 ～ 4 から選びましょう。

1. Its popular products are hats and arm covers.
2. Its paper bags are sold both at home and abroad.
3. Its products are so cheap that even children can buy them.
4. It receives many inquiries about products online.

● Comprehension 2

本文の内容に合うように、1 と 3 の英文を完成させるのに適当なものを、2 の質問の答えとして適当なものを、a ～ d から選びましょう。

1. According to the article, one of washi fabric's notable characteristics is its ability to
a. keep the wearer warmer.
b. amplify the sun's rays.
c. absorb moisture.
d. stick to sweat.

2. Which of the following is a benefit of adding "kumazasa" bamboo grass?
a. It can help neutralize odors.
b. It prevents the fabric from flaking.
c. It cuts the remaining 10% of UV rays.
d. It transforms the tape-like strips into yarn.

3. Hosokawa-Tex, Inc. had to
a. pay SASAWASHI Co. for the rights to use their technology.
b. relocate from Toyama Prefecture to Kobe Prefecture.
c. sell its shoes abroad after failing in the domestic market.
d. create multiple developmental designs of its washi shoes.

Chapter 3

The Secrets of the Ocean Floor

いざ、暗黒の海底へ

Nekton

● Key Expressions 1

CD1-10

音声を聞いて１～３の（　　）内に適当な語を書き入れましょう。

1. Scientists plan to study (w _ _ _ _ _ _ _) in unexplored waters.
   科学者たちは、未踏の海で野生動物の研究を計画している。

2. The AP will be covering the five-week (e _ _ _ _ _ _ _ _ _) into uncharted territory.
   AP 通信は、5 週間にわたる未開の地への探査を取材する予定だ。

3. Professor Laffoley, a marine expert, says it is (c _ _ _ _ _ _ _) to see what's happening in the deep ocean.
   海洋専門家のラフォリー教授は、深海で何が起こっているかを知ることが重要だと述べる。

● Key Expressions 2

以下の１～６の名詞の日本語訳をａ～ｆの選択肢から選び、［　　］内に書き入れましょう。また、動詞形を本文の中から探し出し、その動詞の原形を（　　）内に書き入れましょう。

1. preparation [　　] (　　　　　　)
2. findings [　　] (　　　　　　)
3. completion [　　] (　　　　　　)
4. descent [　　] (　　　　　　)
5. combination [　　] (　　　　　　)
6. presentation [　　] (　　　　　　)

a. 発表	**b.** 組み合わせ	**c.** 準備	**d.** 完了	**e.** 発見	**f.** 降下

● Key Expressions 3

日本語訳を参考に、１～４の（　　）内に適当な前置詞を選択肢から選び、書き入れましょう。ただし、それぞれの前置詞は一回しか使えません。

1. The five-week expedition is targeting seamounts—vast underwater mountains that rise thousands of meters (　　　　　　) the sea floor.
5週間の探査では、海山、つまり海底から数千メートルの高さにある水中の巨大な山を対象としている。

2. Scientists will board one (　　　　　　) the world's most advanced submersibles.
科学者たちは、世界最先端の潜水艇の一つに乗り込む予定だ。

3. When we think of the living space (　　　　　　) the planet for species, over 90% of it is in the ocean.
私たちが地球上に存在する生物種の生活空間を考えると、その90%以上が海中に存在する。

4. They plan to present their findings (　　　　　　) 2022.
彼らは、2022年に研究成果を発表することを計画している。

of	on	from	in

● Background Knowledge

ネクトンミッションの海底探査について、英文に述べられていないものを1～4から選びましょう。

To withstand crushing pressures, the submarine's two-person crew compartment is wrapped in a nine-centimeter (3.5-inch) titanium cocoon. It also carries up to 96 hours' worth of emergency oxygen.

"There are only five vehicles in the world that can get below 6,000 meters (19,685 feet), and this is the only one that goes beyond 8,500 meters," said expedition leader Rob McCallum. "So everything we do is new. Everything we see is virtually a new discovery." Using sampling, sensor and mapping technology, scientists expect to identify new species and towering seamounts, as well as observe man-made impacts, such as climate change and plastic pollution.

The Associated Press

Note seamount「海山（深海底から1,000m以上高くそびえている孤立した海底火山）」

1. （海底探査に使用された）潜水艦は、最大96時間分の非常用酸素を搭載している。
2. 探査隊リーダーのロブ・マッカラム氏によると、6,000メートル（19,685フィート）よりも深い所に到達できる潜水艦は世界で1台もない。
3. 科学者たちは、サンプリング、センサー、マッピング技術を用いて、海山を特定する。
4. 科学者たちは、プラスチック汚染などの人為的な影響を観察することも期待している。

● Newspaper English

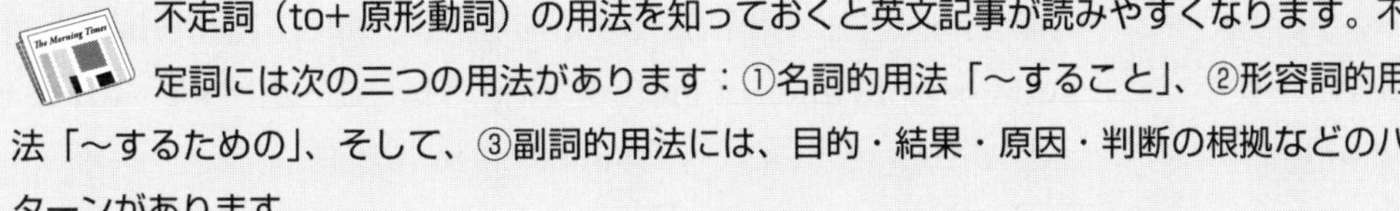

不定詞（to+原形動詞）の用法を知っておくと英文記事が読みやすくなります。不定詞には次の三つの用法があります：①名詞的用法「～すること」、②形容詞的用法「～するための」、そして、③副詞的用法には、目的・結果・原因・判断の根拠などのパターンがあります。

不定詞の用法に気を付けながら、以下の1と2の英文の下線部分の和訳を完成させましょう。

1. A team of scientists decided <u>to dive</u> deep into the depths of the Indian Ocean.
   科学者たちのチームは、インド洋の深海に深く（　　　　　　　　　　）を決意した。
2. <u>To explore</u> such inhospitable depths, Nekton scientists will board "Limiting Factor."
   ネクトンの科学者たちは、そのような人を寄せ付けない深海を（　　　　　　　　　　）、「リミッティング・ファクター」に乗り込む予定だ。

Scientists dive into "Midnight Zone" to study dark ocean

BARCELONA, Spain—A team of scientists is preparing to dive deep into the depths of the Indian Ocean—into a "Midnight Zone" where light barely reaches but life still thrives.

Scientists from the British-led Nekton Mission plan to survey wildlife and gauge the effects of climate change in the unexplored area. Working with the Seychelles and Maldives governments, the five-week expedition is targeting seamounts—vast underwater mountains that rise thousands of meters from the sea floor.

To explore such inhospitable depths, Nekton scientists will board one of the world's most advanced submersibles, called "Limiting Factor."

"What we do know is that beneath 1,000 meters (3,280 feet), there's no light down there, but a lot of animals ... are bioluminescent. It's life that glows," says Nekton mission director Oliver Steeds.

"The area that we're going to be researching, it's one of the most bio-diverse parts of the world's oceans. So what we're going to find there is unknown," Steeds recently told The Associated Press in Barcelona, Spain, before sea trials for the submersible and its mother ship. The AP will be covering the expedition exclusively from start to finish.

Last August, the "Limiting Factor" completed the Five Deeps Expedition, diving to the deepest point in each of the world's five oceans. The deepest was almost 11,000 meters (36,000 feet) down—deeper than Mount Everest is tall.

Last May, when "Limiting Factor" descended to the bottom of the Pacific Ocean's Mariana Trench, the ocean's deepest point, its pilot spotted a plastic bag.

"When we actually think of the living space on the planet for species, over 90% of that living space is in the ocean and

barely「ほとんど～ない」
thrive「生育する」
gauge...「～を判断する」
beneath...「～の下に」
bioluminescent「生物発光の」
bio-diverse「生物多様性に富んだ」
sea trials「海上試運転」
mother ship「母艦」
exclusively「独占的に」
descend「降下する」
trench「海溝」
spot...「～を発見する」

most of that ocean is unexplored," says Dan Laffoley, a marine expert for the International Union for Conservation of Nature.

"So it's absolutely critical, at this time when we see such large changes occurring, that we get people down there, we get eyes in the ocean and we see what's happening," he said.

Scientists will combine their observations with those conducted last year during a seven-week Indian Ocean mission. They plan to present their findings in 2022.

The Associated Press

observation「観測結果」
conduct...「～を行う」

● Summary

以下の空所 1 ～ 4 に当てはまる語を選択肢から選び、書き入れましょう。

A team of scientists is preparing to (1.   ) the deepest areas of the Indian Ocean using advanced technology. Very little is known about the deep oceans, where the only light is produced by the creatures that (2.   ) there. It is hoped that the expedition will (3.   ) humans understand the biodiversity and ecosystems that exist near the ocean floor and the effects that human activity is having on them. The results of these observations will (4.   ) combined with data from similar projects and published in 2022.

be	explore	live	help

● Comprehension 1

本文の内容に合うように、以下の１～４の英文を完成させるのに適当なものをａ～ｄから選び、(　　) 内に書き入れましょう。

1. The goal of the Nekton Mission is to (　　　).
2. The AP will be (　　　).
3. The "Limiting Factor" (　　　).
4. Dan Laffoley says (　　　).

a. covering the Nekton Mission's expedition
b. survey wildlife and climate change effects
c. most of the ocean is unexplored
d. completed the Five Deeps Expedition

● Comprehension 2

本文の内容に合うように、１の質問の答えとして適当なものを、２と３の英文を完成させるのに適当なものを、ａ～ｄから選びましょう。

1. Where is the team leading the Nekton Mission from?
a. Spain
b. Great Britain
c. The Seychelles
d. The Maldives

2. According to Oliver Steeds, the area they will research boasts
a. a wide variety of lifeforms.
b. the world's tallest seamounts.
c. bioluminescent submersibles.
d. a number of limiting factors.

3. According to Dan Laffoley,
a. climate change accounts for 90% of the changes they have observed.
b. we should be more critical about people exploring the deep oceans.
c. most of the planet's habitable areas can be found under water.
d. many of the animals they discovered did not have a need for eyes.

Chapter 4

What Messages Resonate with You?

あなたの心に灯をともします

Hokkeji Temple

● Key Expressions 1

CD1-14

音声を聞いて１～３の（　）内に適当な語を書き入れましょう。

1. Messages on bulletin boards at temples have recently been changing to become more (a _ _ _ _ _ _ _ _ _ _ _).
お寺の掲示板のメッセージが最近、より親しみやすいものに変化してきている。

2. The profile of temple bulletin boards has also been (r _ _ _ _ _), and contests with photo images of their messages are held.
お寺の掲示板の注目度も高まっており、メッセージの画像のコンテストが開かれている。

3. People who visit the temple often take photos of the messages and (f _ _ _ _ _ _) them to others via social media.
このお寺を訪れる人は、しばしばこういったメッセージを写真に撮り、ソーシャルメディアを通じて他の人に送っている。

● Key Expressions 2

以下の１～５は本文に出てくる語句です。英文の定義をａ～ｅより選びましょう。

1. passerby [ ]
2. precept [ ]
3. temple [ ]
4. contest [ ]
5. bulletin board [ ]

a. a principle intended especially as a general rule of action
b. a board to put notices on
c. a person who happens to walk past something
d. a building for religious worship
e. an event in which people compete

● Key Expressions 3

日本語訳を参考に、次の英文の（　）内に入る語句を選択肢より選び、必要なら形を変えて書き入れましょう。

1. Buddhist priest brothers of the Hokkeji temple ( ) photos in summer 2017 with the bulletin board between them.
法華寺の兄弟の僧侶が、間に掲示板を挟んだ写真を、2017年の夏に投稿し始めた。

2. The messages chosen by the two vary widely, ( ) a quotation from Mahatma Gandhi, the father of India's independence, to lyrics of a song ( ) the Japanese rock band The Blue Hearts.
二人が選んだメッセージは多岐にわたり、インド独立の父マハトマ・ガンジーの引用から、日本のロックバンド、ザ・ブルーハーツの歌う歌の歌詞に至るまで様々である。

3. The messages do seem to ( ) inspiration, as visitors said that they were encouraged by them.
この寺を訪れた人がそのようなメッセージに元気づけられたと言っているため、そのメッセージは実際にインスピレーションとなっているようである。

sing by	serve as	range from	begin posting

● Background Knowledge

CD1-15

お寺の掲示板について、英文に述べられていないものを１～４から選びましょう。

Temples putting up a bulletin board in front of their gates and propagating the Buddhist teachings is called "preaching via notice," and it is said to date back to the Meiji era (1868–1912). This long-standing practice drew particular attention after Bukkyo Dendo Kyokai (the Society for the Promotion of Buddhism)—a public interest incorporated foundation—launched the "Kagayake! Otera-no-Keijiban Taisho" (Shine! The Temples' Bulletin Boards Grand Prize) in 2018. In a bid to give ordinary people the opportunity to experience Buddhism, the society invited people to send in photos of temples' bulletin boards via social media.

The Japan News

Notes propagate...「～を伝える」　notice「貼り紙」　in a bid to...「～しようとして」

1. お寺の掲示板の慣習は明治時代に始まったと言われている。
2. この掲示板への貼り紙が注目されたのはあるコンテストがきっかけであった。
3. このコンテストの目的は一般の人に仏教を体験する機会を与えることである。
4. 仏教伝道協会はお寺の掲示板に載せるメッセージを一般の人々より募集している。

● Newspaper English

新聞記事によっては、関連する写真と写真の説明文（キャプション）があるものもあり、記事の内容理解を助けてくれます。

以下の写真についているキャプションの（　　）内に入る適当な語句をａ～ｃの選択肢より選びましょう。

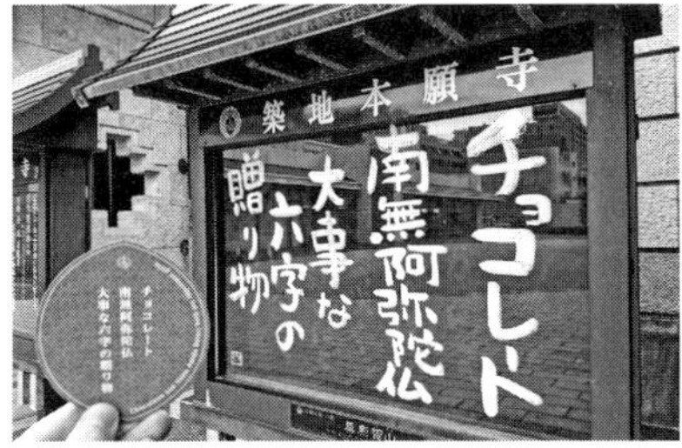

The Yomiuri Shimbun

The bulletin board at the Tsukiji Hongwanji temple in Tokyo. The messages are written by officials of the temple. Left (　　) is a commemorative card for visiting the temple.

a. at the front in the photo
b. in front of the photo
c. under the roof of the bulletin board

Comeback of temple bulletin boards

Bulletin boards at temples, which usually have serious messages like precepts for living or Buddhist phrases, have recently been changing to become more approachable, with expressions that are expected to attract the attention of ordinary people.

The use of such messages has become increasingly popular, as these words may prompt temple visitors or passersby to think about their life. The profile of temple bulletin boards has also been rising. For instance, contests with photo images of the messages are held and the ones that resonate with the most people are awarded.

"Chocolate (written using six katakana characters), Namu Amida Butsu (translated as 'I sincerely believe in Amida Buddha'): Precious Gifts in Six Characters." That is the message that is posted this month on the bulletin board at the Tsukiji Hongwanji in Chuo Ward, Tokyo. According to the temple, the phrase 'Namu Amida Butsu' (which is denoted in six kanji) is a gift containing the mindfulness of the Buddha, just as chocolate will be given as a present on Saint Valentine's Day. The phrase was chosen by temple officials who have been ordained to the priesthood.

In recent years, the temple has increasingly been using messages expressed in plain words, such as: "We offer our thanks not because we are happy. Our being able to offer thanks is where we can find our happiness" and "We can change neither others' nor our past, but we can change ourselves and our future."

As the people who visit the temple often take photos of these messages and forward them to others via social media, the messages have become a topic of conversation.

Starting this month, the temple has also made an effort to explain the messages on its "commemorative card for visiting the temple," which is distributed to visitors free of charge. It

prompt...to ~「…に~するよう促す」

resonate with...「~の心に響く」

denote...「~を表す」

be ordained to the priesthood「仏門に入る」

commemorative「記念の」

distribute...「~を配る」

is written not only in Japanese but also in English. Kazuki Kitamoto, an official in charge of public relations, said, "We would be pleased if those who casually drop in for a short visit feel something resonate with them, thus deepening their ties with our temple."

The Japan News

public relations「広報」
drop in...「〜に立ち寄る」

Summary

CD1-17

以下の空所１〜４に当てはまる語を選択肢から選び、書き入れましょう。

In an effort to attract and engage (1.   ) visitors, some Japanese temples have started to change their approach to the (2.   ) bulletin board found outside. Using (3.   ) language and drawing links between Buddhist teachings and features of modern-day life, such messages have struck a chord with many people, and have increasingly been posted to and shared on (4.   ) media.

simple	traditional	new	social

● Comprehension 1

本文の内容に当てはまるように、与えられた頭文字から始まる語を書き入れ、文章を完成させましょう。

1. Bulletin boards at temples usually have (s _ _ _ _ _ _) messages, such as precepts for living or Buddhist phrases.

2. Increasingly, messages are being expressed in (p _ _ _ _) words.

3. These words on the boards make visitors and (p _ _ _ _ _ _ _ _) think about their lives.

4. Such messages have become a (t _ _ _ _) of conversation.

● Comprehension 2

本文の内容に合うように、1と3の質問の答えとして適当なものを、2の英文を完成させるのに適当なものを、a〜dから選びましょう。

1. What is the purpose of the messages on the temple bulletin boards?

a. To advertise the temple's services
b. To inform people about changes to the temple
c. To promote the temple's social media accounts
d. To make people reflect on their lives

2. The message likening chocolate to belief in Amida Buddha was written by

a. Saint Valentine.
b. visitors to Tsukiji Hongwanji.
c. temple priests.
d. social media consultants.

3. What does Kazuki Kitamoto hope will happen?

a. Foreign visitors will start to pay for commemorative cards.
b. The messages will be translated into more languages.
c. The temple will return to posting more traditional messages.
d. Visitors will develop stronger relationships with his temple.

Chapter 5

Let's Change the World from #KuToo

「苦痛」のない社会を目指して「靴」からできる第一歩

AFP-JIJI

Key Expressions 1

CD1-18

音声を聞いて1～3の（　　）内に適当な語を書き入れましょう。

1. Ms. Yumi Ishikawa wants to stop the culture of (r _ _ _ _ _ _ _ _) women to wear high heels at work.
石川優実さんは、女性に職場でハイヒールを履かせる文化を止めたいと考えている。

2. The phrase #KuToo is a (c _ _ _ _ _ _ _ _ _ _) of the Japanese word *kutsu*, meaning shoes, and *kutsuu*, meaning pain.
#KuTooという言葉は、日本語の「靴」と痛みを意味する「苦痛」を組み合わせたものだ。

3. The #KuToo movement is aiming to end (d _ _ _ _ _ _ _ _ _ _ _ _ _) against women.
#KuToo運動は、女性差別をなくすことを目指している。

● Key Expressions 2

接頭辞 re- には、again（再び）や back（後ろへ）という意味を付け加える働きがあります。

枠内の説明を参考に、以下の１～５の単語の意味を選択肢から選び、（　　）内に書き入れましょう。

1. reiterate　　(　　　　　　　　)
2. recall　　(　　　　　　　　)
3. recline　　(　　　　　　　　)
4. reconstruct　　(　　　　　　　　)
5. reverse　　(　　　　　　　　)

寄り掛かる	逆にする	繰り返し言う	再建する	思い出す

● Key Expressions 3

英語での数字の読み方にはいくつかのルールがあります。大きな桁の数は、「下 3 桁ごと」に区切って読みます。西暦は、前半と後半の 2 桁ずつに分けて読みます。ただし、「2010 年以降」は 2 桁ずつに区切って読むパターンと、thousand を使うパターンの 2 種類があり、どちらとも使われています。

以下の１と２の下線部の数字の読み方を、例のようにつづりで書きましょう。

例： Ms. Ishikawa is 33 years old.
(thirty-three)

1. About 32,000 people signed the petition.
(　　　　　　　　　　　　　　　　)

2. #KuToo was selected as one of the 10 most memorable buzzwords in Japan in 2019.
2 桁ずつに区切って読むパターン：
(　　　　　　　　　　　　　　　　)
thousand を使うパターン：
(　　　　　　　　　　　　　　　　)

● Background Knowledge

#KuToo に対する企業の反応について、英文に述べられていないものを１～４から選びましょう。

Corporate Japan has not exactly embraced #KuToo, although there are exceptions. The cosmetics company Orbis has supported the movement and encourages staff to dress as they like at work, according to Ishikawa. The cellphone operator Docomo changed its dress code last year so women weren't forced to wear high heels, but it said the shift was not prompted by the movement.

"Businesses probably see the issue of discrimination as women talking about something annoying," Ishikawa said. "They tend to shy away from it, seeing us as radical, but on our part, we think we are not saying anything controversial."

The Washington Post

Notes radical「急進的な」 controversial「論争の的になる」

1. 例外はあるものの、日本の企業は #KuToo 運動を正確には受け入れているわけではない。
2. 化粧品会社のオルビスは、#KuToo 運動を支持していない。
3. 携帯電話会社のドコモは、女性にハイヒールを無理に履かせないよう服装規定を変更した。
4. 石川さんには、女性が何か面倒なことを話しているかのごとく企業が差別問題を捉えているようにうつる。

● Newspaper English

英字新聞のヘッドライン（見出し）は、通常の英語とは少し異なるルールで作られています。代表的なのは、時制です。過去の出来事でも現在形で書いたり、「to ＋動詞の原形」で未来の出来事を表したりします。また、冠詞が省略されることもあります。

以下の１と２のヘッドラインの（　　）内に当てはまる動詞を選択肢から選び、適当な形に変化させて書き入れましょう。

1. Ms. Ishikawa (　　　　　　　　　　) new website next month
   石川氏、来月新しいウェブサイトを立ち上げ
2. #MeToo movement (　　　　　　　　　　) backlash
   #MeToo 運動、反発を呼ぶ

prompt	launch

In Japan, a campaign against high heels targets conformity and discrimination

A year ago, Yumi Ishikawa, 33, came home from her job at a funeral services company, her feet hurting and bleeding, and tweeted out a message to the world. “I want to stop this culture of requiring women to wear high heels and pumps at work,” the former model wrote. “Why do we have to work with our feet injured while men are wearing flat shoes?”

From that tweet, a movement was born, christened #KuToo in a nod to the #MeToo movement. The phrase is also a play on the Japanese word *kutsu*, meaning shoes, and *kutsuu*, meaning pain.

It prompted a backlash on social media from both men and women, as well as insults and abuse for Ishikawa, but also a petition signed by nearly 32,000 people that has challenged Japan’s culture of conformity to societal expectations and deeply embedded gender discrimination.

Selected as one of the 10 most memorable buzzwords in Japan in 2019, #KuToo may not have changed the way many Japanese women are required to dress at work, but it has afforded them a new voice.

“I’m having a great time,” said Ishikawa, who describes herself as an actress, writer and feminist, in a recent interview just before the launch of a website designed to bring new structure to the movement. “I don’t see myself as a leader. But just like acting, this is a way to express myself.”

Ishikawa’s own message—that women should have the same footwear choices as men—has not always been well received in Japan’s conservative, don’t-rock-the-boat society. It is not a question, she patiently reiterates, of telling women they can’t wear high heels, or even suggesting they should be allowed to wear sneakers, but an attempt to “level the playing field” so women are not forced by corporate dress codes to conform to a different standard from men.

conformity「服従」
bleed「血を流す」
christen...「～に命名する」
in a nod to...「～に呼応して」
a play on the word「言葉遊び」
insult「侮辱」
petition「嘆願書」
embedded「根付いた」
buzzword「流行語」
afford...「～を与える」
launch「開設」
conservative「保守的な」
don't-rock-the-boat「事なかれ主義」
level the playing field「平等な条件にする」
conform to...「～に従う」

In Japan, people such as Ishikawa are often branded "activists," as a way of marginalizing their messages. It is a label she rejects.

Still, her ultimate goal is not just to secure the freedom to wear the same shoes as men for women in Japan. It is to end discrimination against them more broadly.

The Washington Post

brand...「～であるとレッテルを貼る」
marginalize...「～を排除する」

Summary

CD1-21

以下の空所１～４に当てはまる語を選択肢から選び、書き入れましょう。

One woman's (1.   ), highlighting the pain of being forced by Japanese corporate culture to wear high heels, has led to a social movement for (2.   ) gathering around the hashtag #KuToo. Despite some (3.   ) and online trolling, the movement has gathered tens of thousands of signatures in support and #KuToo was recognized as one of the top buzzwords of 2019. The broader goals of the movement are to highlight and challenge gender (4.   ) in the Japanese workplace, leveling the playing field for women and men.

equality	tweet	inequality	backlash

● Comprehension 1

石川さんのとった言動に当てはまるものを、1～4の英文から一つ選びましょう。

1. She started the #MeToo movement to oppose society.
2. She changed the dress code of all companies.
3. She tweeted out a message after she came home from her job.
4. She described herself as an activist in an interview.

● Comprehension 2

本文の内容に合うように、1と3の英文を完成させるのに適当なものを、2の質問の答えとして適当なものを、a～dから選びましょう。

1. In part, the movement was named "#KuToo" because
  a. the leaders of the #MeToo movement suggested that name.
  b. Ishikawa didn't want to be sued for copyright infringement.
  c. it invokes two similar sounding and relevant Japanese words.
  d. it is the title of a famous play about gender inequality.

2. Which of the following statements is true?
  a. Ishikawa claims many women cannot afford high heels.
  b. Ishikawa received almost 32,000 abusive messages.
  c. #KuToo was the tenth most popular hashtag in 2019.
  d. People of both genders have opposed the movement.

3. Ishikawa believes that
  a. men and women should be given the same opportunities and choices.
  b. women should stop wearing high heels as a form of protest.
  c. the term "activist" should be reclaimed and celebrated.
  d. official corporate dress codes should be made illegal.

Chapter 6

Spiders Will Change the Fashion Industry

夢の材料

The Asahi Shimbun

● Key Expressions 1

CD1-22

音声を聞いて１～３の（　　）内に適当な語を書き入れましょう。

1. Strands of spider silk have (p _ _ _ _ _ _ _ _ _) that offer a host of commercial applications.
   クモ糸は多数の商業的な応用ができる特性を持つ。

2. A young Japanese entrepreneur has successfully produced (s _ _ _ _ _ _ _ _) spider silk after a 15-year effort.
   ある若い日本人起業家が、15 年努力したのちに、見事に人工クモ糸を生み出した。

3. This fiber, called "Brewed Protein™," has attracted attention as a groundbreaking material because it is not (d _ _ _ _ _ _) from petroleum.
   「ブリュード・プロテイン」と呼ばれるこの繊維は、石油由来ではないという理由から、革新的な素材であるとして注目を集めている。

● Key Expressions 2

以下の１～７は人工クモ糸に関する語句です。日本語訳を選択肢から選び、（　　）内に書き入れましょう。

1. gene (　　　　　　　　)
2. amino acid (　　　　　　　　)
3. sequence (　　　　　　　　)
4. fermentation (　　　　　　　　)
5. sustainable (　　　　　　　　)
6. flexible (　　　　　　　　)
7. durable (　　　　　　　　)

耐久性のある	発酵	アミノ酸	遺伝子	配列	持続可能な	柔軟な

● Key Expressions 3

日本語訳を参考に、以下の１～３の英文の（　　）内に適当な表現を選択肢から選び、書き入れましょう。

1. Spiber Inc., headquartered in Tsuruoka, Yamagata Prefecture, has 224 employees, (　　　　　　　　) 30 percent are locals. Ten percent of its employees are from outside Japan.
Spiber 株式会社は、山形県鶴岡市に本社があり、224 名の社員がいる（2020 年時点）。そのうちの 30%が地元出身者で、社員の 10%は国外出身者である。

2. The first shipments from the Thai factory will be in 2021, and the company's production volume is expected to increase (　　　　　　　　) from (　　　　　　　　).
タイの工場からの最初の出荷は 2021 年になると予想され、この企業の生産量は現在の 5 メートルトンから 100 倍に増えると予測されている。

3. Spiber owns (　　　　　　　　) 240 patents, including those pending.
Spiber 株式会社は未決定のものも含めて 240 以上もの特許を所有している。

100-fold	more than	of whom	the current 5 tonnes

Background Knowledge

人工クモ糸を開発したSpiber株式会社の取締役兼代表執行役の関山氏の開発秘話について、英文に述べられていないものを1～4から選びましょう。

Kazuhide Sekiyama's light bulb moment to pursue spider silk research came during a conversation he had during a drinking session with fellow students at Keio University, where he majored in environment and information studies.

He recalled that his friends started talking about the "strongest" insect. One member of the party plumped for hornets because of their poisonous sting. But the group concluded spiders must be stronger because they capture hornets in their webs. Inspired, Sekiyama wasted no time in collecting several dozen spiders in a mountain area near the university and devouring academic publications to bone up on the issue.

The Asahi Shimbun

Notes plump for...「～を支持する」 bone up on...「～について猛勉強する」

1. 関山氏は人工クモ糸の研究のアイデアを仲間との飲み会でひらめいた。
2. 彼は大学で環境情報学を専攻していた。
3. 彼は山中でクモの巣にスズメバチがかかっているのをたまたま見た。
4. 彼は思いついたらすぐにクモを集めたり、文献を読みあさったりした。

Newspaper English

新聞では記事を印象深いものにするために、テーマにまつわる比喩表現を用いたり、比較級などを用いて事実を強調したりすることがあります。

以下の1と2の（　）内に適当な語句を選び、必要なら形を変えて書き入れましょう。

1. A young Japanese entrepreneur has (　　　　　　　　　　) after a 15-year effort to produce synthetic spider silk.
   ある若い日本人起業家が、人工クモ糸を生み出すのに15年努力したのちに、金を紡ぎだした（大きな成果を得た）。

2. Sekiyama's timing could not (　　　　　　　　　　) as the fashion industry is under increasing pressure to produce sustainable products.
   ファッション業界が持続可能な製品を作るよう次第に圧力をかけられている中、関山氏のタイミングはまたとないものであった。

be better　　spin gold

● Reading

Groundbreaking material: synthetic spider silk

A young Japanese entrepreneur has spun gold after a 15-year effort to produce synthetic spider silk, something U.S. and European companies have long tried to achieve.

The payoff is this: strands of spider silk are stronger than steel and more flexible than nylon, properties that offer a host of commercial applications.

Kazuhide Sekiyama, 36, said his dream fiber, called "Brewed Protein™," is now being put to practical use.

He started out by analyzing spider genes and used his own technology to synthesize genes that can produce proteins with amino acid sequences tailored for specific usage. Proteins are produced through fermentation by micro-organisms injected with the genes. The proteins are then refined and assembled into fibers.

This past June, popular Japanese fashion brand Sacai showed off T-shirts made with Brewed Protein™ threads during Paris Men's Fashion Week.

Another Japanese brand, YUIMA NAKAZATO, also used the newly developed material woven into a fabric similar to silk satin for its entire couture collection.

Sekiyama's timing could not be better as the fashion industry is under increasing pressure to produce sustainable products.

Brewed Protein™ has attracted attention as a groundbreaking material because it is not derived from petroleum. Sekiyama said he has received a string of offers from famous European brands.

In 2007, at the age of 24, he set up a start-up company called Spiber Inc.

In 2015, Spiber collaborated with sports apparel manufacturer Goldwin Inc. on a joint research and

payoff「報酬」
synthesize...「〜を合成する」
tailor... for ~「〜のために…を改造する」
inject...「〜を注入する」
assemble... into ~「…を〜に生成する」
weave...「〜を織る」
a string of...「続々と」

development project to improve the strength, flexibility and durability of the fibers.

The material is being touted for a range of fields, including automobiles, medical care, architecture and space development.

In December, Goldwin is set to release an outdoor jacket called the Moon Parka from its brand, The North Face, that utilizes Brewed Protein™.

The Asahi Shimbun

be touted for...「〜に宣伝される」

● Summary

CD1-25

以下の空所１～４に当てはまる語を選択肢から選び、書き入れましょう。ただし、文頭に来る語も小文字で与えられています。

After many years of effort, a Japanese entrepreneur has succeeded in producing a (1.   ) form of spider silk. The (2.   ) potential for the material, Brewed Protein™, is high. (3.   ) manufacturers might also be attracted by the fact that Brewed Protein™ is not derived from petroleum. It has already been incorporated into the collections of (4.   ) fashion brands, and it is likely to find applications in other fields, too.

synthetic	eco-minded	commercial	several

● Comprehension 1

本文の内容に当てはまるものにはT（True）を、当てはまらないものにはF（False）を、1～4の（　）内に書き入れましょう。

1. It took more than a decade for Sekiyama to succeed in producing their synthetic form of spider silk. (　　)

2. Two Japanese brands already use Spiber's synthetic spider silk. (　　)

3. European brands are also interested in Brewed Protein™. (　　)

4. Spiber Inc. and Goldwin Inc. are trying to produce much stronger, more flexible and durable products than the Moon Parka. (　　)

● Comprehension 2

本文の内容に合うように、1と3の質問の答えとして適当なものを、2の英文を完成させるのに適当なものを、a～dから選びましょう。

1. What was the first step in Sekiyama's development process?

a. He analyzed the structural properties of nylon.
b. He went abroad to continue his education in the field.
c. He applied for a commercial license to begin trials.
d. He studied the genetic makeup of a silk-producing animal.

2. The article suggests that the timing of the product's development is good because

a. many people are opening up to the idea of eating spiders and other arachnids.
b. the fashion industry is being urged to reduce its environmental impact.
c. at least two Japanese brands have vowed to stop using petroleum-derived fabrics.
d. the theme of a recent prestigious Men's Fashion Week was "organic."

3. Which potential use of the product is NOT suggested in the article?

a. In aerospace engineering
b. As a building material
c. As a foodstuff
d. In vehicle construction

Chapter 7

Sharp Decline in Butterfly Population

里山のチョウが絶滅の危機

Masakazu Takahashi (left) / Katsuhiko Yokoi, Okutama Support Park Ranger Association (right)

● Key Expressions 1

CD1-26

音声を聞いて１～３の（　　）内に適当な語を書き入れましょう。

1. Butterflies react very quickly to environmental changes, making them excellent indicators of (b _ _ _ _ _ _ _ _ _ _ _).
チョウは環境変化に非常に素早く反応し、そのことがチョウを生物多様性の優れた指標としている。

2. Of 87 (s _ _ _ _ _ _) of butterfly, about 40% were rapidly decreasing in number.
87種のチョウのうち、およそ40パーセントの数が急激に減っていた。

3. About 1,000 people interested in nature conservation activities (p _ _ _ _ _ _ _ _ _ _) in the annual monitoring activities.
自然保護活動に興味を持つおよそ1,000人が、毎年の監視活動に参加している。

● Key Expressions 2

bio- は「生物」「生命」を表す接頭辞です。先端技術と結びついて、今後も bio を含む語は増えていくことが見込まれます。ぜひ覚えて活用しましょう。

枠内の接頭辞の説明を参考に、以下の１～６の日本語に該当する語を選択肢から選び、(　　) 内に書き入れましょう。

1. 生物学 (　　　　　　　　　　)
2. 生化学 (　　　　　　　　　　)
3. 生物多様性 (　　　　　　　　　　)
4. 生物燃料 (　　　　　　　　　　)
5. 伝記 (　　　　　　　　　　)
6. 生物学的災害 (　　　　　　　　　　)

biochemistry	biohazard	biofuel
biology	biodiversity	biography

● Key Expressions 3

英語では長い主語は好ましくないと言われていますが、論説文においては、実はそれほど珍しくありません。以下の１～３の文の主語にあたる部分に下線を引きましょう。

1. Drops in the number of species of plants and animals have become a worldwide concern.

2. The loss of biodiversity and related changes in the environment are now faster than ever before in human history.

3. Rapid destruction of wild habitats for farming and urbanization is likely to be significantly reducing the number of insects.

● Background Knowledge

里山における外来種の影響について、英文に述べられていないものを１～４から選びましょう。

The spawning of montane brown frogs in forestry areas in Hanno, Saitama Prefecture, was found to have shrunk from around 2013. Around the same time, a number of raccoons began to be spotted, and they were eventually confirmed to have inhabited the area in 2015. By the end of 2017, four raccoons had been captured in traps, and the frogs' egg production was found to have recovered.

"Although a causal relationship cannot be determined, this is a case in which the influence of a foreign species is strongly suspected," an expert said.

The Japan News

Notes montane brown frog「ヤマアカガエル」 causal relationship「因果関係」

1. 飯能市の緑地でのヤマアカガエルの産卵数が 2013 年頃から減少したことがわかった。
2. 飯能市の緑地に生息するアライグマの数も 2013 年頃から減り始めた。
3. 2017 年には、ヤマアカガエルの産卵数が回復したことがわかった。
4. 外来種が在来種の産卵数に影響を与えた疑いが強いことが明らかになった。

● Newspaper English

英字新聞では自明の事柄は省略されることが多いですが、とくに副詞節を導く接続詞節内では、文脈から自明の主語と動詞がしばしば省略されます。

以下の１～３の（　　）内に省略された語句を、書き入れましょう。

1. They recorded the species and populations of living creatures they encountered while (　　　　　　　　　　) walking predetermined routes.

2. When (　　　　　　　　　　) asked if they had heard about biodiversity, about 70 percent of the students said yes.

3. If (　　　　　　　　　　) possible, the professor wants to participate in the survey himself.

Survey finds sharp drop in butterfly numbers

Drops in the number of species of plants and animals have become a worldwide concern, and a survey's findings, released in November, indicate the trend could be also occurring in places close to human communities in Japan.

In 2002, the Environment Ministry compiled the National Biodiversity Strategy of Japan, under which it started a project to continuously monitor the natural environment, so as to conserve it. The Nature Conservation Society of Japan (NACS-J) serves as a secretariat for the project.

About 1,000 people interested in nature conservation activities, including laypersons, students and researchers, participate in the annual monitoring activities. Titled "Monitoring Sites 1,000 Program," the survey got fully underway in fiscal 2008. Participants recorded the species and populations of living creatures they encountered while walking predetermined routes and using cameras that could take automatic pictures.

Analysis of the data showed the number of butterflies has been declining considerably. Among 34 species experiencing such drops, the alpine black swallowtail, which can be found in a wide range of regions from Hokkaido to Kyushu, has decreased by an average of 31.4% per year. The number of great purple emperor, which is designated as the national butterfly of Japan, has fallen 16.1% per year.

When compiling its own red list of species threatened with extinction, the ministry categorizes species based on such factors as how fast they are decreasing in number, how wide their area of habitation is, and how high the danger is of their extinction in the immediate future.

Based on the rates of decline found in the survey, about 40% of the monitored butterflies could be considered endangered species on the red list, according to NACS-J.

"The survey showed once again how critical the butterflies'

findings「結果、発見」
compile...「～を策定する」
the National Biodiversity Strategy「生物多様性国家戦略」
the Nature Conservation Society of Japan「日本自然保護協会」
secretariat「事務局」
layperson「(専門家でない)一般の人」
predetermined「あらかじめ決められた」
alpine black swallowtail「ミヤマカラスアゲハ」
great purple emperor「オオムラサキ」
red list「レッドリスト（絶滅のおそれのある野生生物の種のリスト)」
threatened with extinction「絶滅の危機にひんしている」
categorize...「～を分類する」
habitation「生息」
critical「危機的な」

situation is," said Minoru Ishii, a professor emeritus of insect ecology at Osaka Prefecture University. "Butterflies support ecosystems through the food chain, as their larvae are eaten by other animals. This means their decreasing numbers will have a major impact on other creatures."

In addition to butterflies, the survey found a similar trend among about 20% of bird species covered in the monitoring activities, such as cuckoos. The number of hares also nosedived.

The Japan News

professor emeritus「名誉教授」
larvae「幼虫（larvaの複数形）」
hare「野ウサギ」
nosedive「急激に減る、急降下する」

Summary

以下の空所１～４に当てはまる語を選択肢から選び、書き入れましょう。

A recent Japanese ecological survey, (1.   ) by around one thousand people with an interest in conservation, has (2.   ) worrying declines in the number of several species, including butterflies, birds and hares. Such declines have (3.   ) certain species on the endangered list, and a scientist has (4.   ) that their disappearance could have a devastating effect on the ecosystems of which they are a part.

placed	revealed	warned	conducted

● Comprehension 1

以下の１～４の（　　）内に当てはまる団体名・組織名を選択肢から選び、書き入れましょう。複数回使うものもあります。また、文頭に来る語も小文字で与えられています。

1. (　　　　　　　　　　　　　　　　　　　　) compiled the National Biodiversity Strategy of Japan.
2. Professor Ishii once taught at (　　　　　　　　　　　　　　　　　　　　).
3. The secretariat of the National Biodiversity Strategy of Japan is (　　　　　　　　　　　　　　　　　　　　).
4. (　　　　　　　　　　　　　　　　　　　　) compiles its own red list of species threatened with extinction.

the Environment Ministry　　the Nature Conservation Society of Japan Osaka Prefecture University

● Comprehension 2

本文の内容に合うように、１と３の英文を完成させるのに適当なものを、２の質問の答えとして適当なものを、a～d から選びましょう。

1. The people who conducted the survey had to
   a. have at least one thousand hours of field experience.
   b. gather data from along a set route.
   c. be specialists with qualifications in ecology.
   d. record videos of the animals they encountered.

2. Which of the following is mentioned as a factor used to compile the red list?
   a. The average size of their young as they grow
   b. The number of a species' natural predators
   c. The rate of population decline within a species
   d. The species' status as a national symbol

3. According to Professor Ishii, a decline in the number of butterflies will
   a. create a gap in the ecosystem for non-native species to flourish.
   b. necessitate conducting the survey again with more frequency.
   c. lead to a boom in the number of larvae of other inedible species.
   d. severely affect other animals that typically prey on their larvae.

Chapter 8

Volcanic Ash Attracts Tourists

嫌われものが神業アートに大変身

The Yomiuri Shimbun

● Key Expressions 1

CD1-30

音声を聞いて1～3の（　　）内に適当な語を書き入れましょう。

1. The ash from the volcano on Sakurajima is a source of (c _ _ _ _ _ _) for the people of Kagoshima.
桜島の火山灰は、鹿児島の人々にとって悩みの種である。

2. Kyoko Uemura, a former (e _ _ _ _ _ _ _) of the Sakurajima Visitor Center, works on "volcanic ash art."
桜島ビジターセンター元職員の植村恭子さんは、「火山灰アート」に取り組んでいる。

3. The (p _ _ _ _ _ _ _ _ _) of the volcanic ash art on social media has begun to attract tourists.
ソーシャルメディアにおける火山灰アートの人気が観光客を引き付け始めている。

● Key Expressions 2

動詞を ing 形にする場合、次のような 3 つのパターンがあります。①動詞にそのまま ing を付ける、② e で終わる動詞の場合、e を取って ing を付ける、③「短母音＋子音字」で終わる動詞の場合、最後の子音字を重ねて ing を付ける。

枠内の説明を参考に、以下の 1 ～ 6 の動詞を ing 形に変化させましょう。

1. dry（乾かす）→ [ ]
2. collect（集める）→ [ ]
3. enjoy（楽しむ）→ [ ]
4. make（作る）→ [ ]
5. get（得る）→ [ ]
6. take（取る）→ [ ]

● Key Expressions 3

日本語訳を参考に、以下の 1 ～ 3 の（ ）内に適当な関係代名詞もしくは関係副詞を選び、書き入れましょう。

1. Kyoko Uemura is a former employee of a nonprofit organization ( ) operates the Sakurajima Visitor Center.
植村恭子さんは、桜島ビジターセンターを運営する NPO 法人の元職員である。

2. The Sakurajima Visitor Center is the facility ( ) the history of the volcanic eruption is displayed.
桜島ビジターセンターは、火山の噴火の歴史が展示されている施設である。

3. Saigo Takamori, ( ) played a vital role in the Meiji government, and the Japanese national team, who played well in the Rugby World Cup, are popular motifs.
明治政府で極めて重要な役割を果たした西郷隆盛や、ラグビーワールドカップで活躍した日本代表チームは、人気のモチーフである。

where	that	who

● Background Knowledge

火山灰アーティストの久木田智美さんについて、英文に述べられていないものを１～４から選びましょう。

Processed products using ash have been developed one after another. Tomomi Kukita, 35, makes and sells volcanic ash jewelry in the city. "In Kagoshima, jewels fall from the sky," Kukita—a former colleague from the NPO Kyoko Uemura used to work for—said. When Kukita was thinking of creating a new souvenir, she was fascinated by images of lava magnified with a polarizing microscope. "It was sparkling like a jewel," she said.

The Japan News

Note lava「溶岩」

1. 鹿児島市内で火山灰を使ったジュエリーを作り、販売している。
2. 「鹿児島では宝石が空から降ってくる」と語った。
3. 植村恭子さんとは、かつて別々の NPO 法人で働いていた。
4. 偏光顕微鏡で拡大した溶岩の画像に魅せられた。

● Newspaper English

長さ・重さを示す単位を使う時には、注意点があります。数値が１以外の場合は、単位を複数形にする必要があるので気を付けましょう。例えば、「お茶 50 グラム」であれば、50 grams of teaとなります。ただし、単位にg（グラム）やkg（キログラム）などの記号を用いる時は、複数形にする必要はなく、50 g of tea となります。

以下の１と２の英文には、長さや重さを示す表現が含まれていますが、修正すべきところがあります。どこを直すべきか考え、英文を正しく書きかえましょう。

1. She drew the protagonist from a manga in a wooden frame—1.2 meter by 1.8 meter.

   ____

   彼女は、漫画の主人公を 1.2 メートル×1.8 メートルの木枠の中に描いた。

2. Ms. Uemura used 3 kilogram of sand to draw the "volcanic ash art."

   ____

   植村さんは、その「火山灰アート」を描くのに 3 キロの砂を使った。

Reading

Sakurajima volcanic ash transformed into art

KAGOSHIMA—Sakurajima island is the symbol of Kagoshima. However, the ash from the volcano on the island is a source of concern for local residents as it prevents them from drying laundry outside and it completely covers vehicles. Efforts are being made to turn this “nuisance” into a local resource.

The Sakurajima Visitor Center in the city displays the history of the volcanic eruptions. In front of the entrance, Kyoko Uemura, 36, a former employee of a nonprofit organization that operates the facility, was working on “volcanic ash art.”

Uemura was holding volcanic ash in her right hand after collecting it from the surrounding area. A line was drawn when she sprinkled the ash little by little on the ground. To tie in with a marketing campaign that celebrates Nov. 26 as “Good Bath Day,” she drew the protagonist and another character from a manga about public bathhouses called “Thermae Romae” in a wooden frame—1.2 meters by 1.8 meters—in just 10 minutes.

After strong earthquakes in Kumamoto Prefecture in April 2016, the visitor center launched a fundraising campaign. In order to raise money, Uemura’s colleague suggested that the ash could be used to draw Kumamoto Prefecture’s mascot Kumamon. She liked drawing anime characters, so she took up the challenge.

The width of the lines and depth of the color varies depending on the amount of ash used for the drawing and the height from which the ash is carefully scattered. The theme of the drawings varies as well. Saigo Takamori, who played a vital role in the Meiji government, and the Japanese national team who played well in the Rugby World Cup were popular motifs.

Sometimes Uemura draws visitors. When these visitors

nuisance「迷惑なもの」
tie in with...「~に合わせる」
public bathhouse「公衆浴場」
launch...「~を始める」
colleague「同僚」
take up the challenge「挑戦する」
scatter...「~をまき散らす」

posted her portraits of them on social media, it made more people want to go see the volcanic ash art.

Uemura now works as a "volcanic ash artist." She said, "This art form was created because we are in close proximity to the volcano. I'm happy if this encourages people to become interested in Sakurajima."

The Japan News

proximity「近接」

● Summary

以下の空所１～４に当てはまる語を選択肢から選び、書き入れましょう。

A local Kagoshima woman has (1.   ) a novel way of attracting visitors to the city's famous volcano, Sakurajima. Although the volcano's ash is often (2.   ) a nuisance by those living in its shadow, Kyoko Uemura uses it to create portraits of famous people, well-known characters and even the visitors themselves. Uemura's "volcanic ash art" has proved popular with visitors, who have (3.   ) it on social media. It has now (4.   ) an attraction itself!

become	shared	found	considered

● Comprehension 1

本文の内容に合うように、以下の１～５の英文の（　　）内に入る適当な語を選択肢より選び、書き入れましょう。

1. Efforts are being (　　　　　　　　　　) to turn their "nuisance" into a local resource.

2. A line was (　　　　　　　　　　) when Uemura sprinkled the ash little by little on the ground.

3. Nov. 26 is (　　　　　　　　　　) as "Good Bath Day."

4. The ash was carefully (　　　　　　　　　　) by Uemura.

5. The ash art was (　　　　　　　　　　) because Uemura is in close proximity to the volcano.

drawn	scattered	created	known	made

● Comprehension 2

本文の内容に合うように、１と２の英文を完成させるのに適当なものを、３の質問の答えとして適当なものを、a～d から選びましょう。

1. According to the article, because of the ash, local residents sometimes

a. are prevented from accessing local resources.
b. cannot dry their washing outdoors.
c. are unable to purchase insurance cover for their cars.
d. cannot see the city's famous symbol.

2. When the journalist arrived, Kyoko Uemura was

a. sprinkling ash into a bath as part of a marketing campaign.
b. explaining the history of the volcano to some visitors.
c. researching her next design by reading manga.
d. working just outside of the Sakurajima Visitor Center.

3. What was the subject of Uemura's first attempt at drawing with volcanic ash?

a. A famous person from political history
b. The volcano itself
c. A well-known local mascot
d. One of her now ex-coworkers

Chapter 9

Seeking Work-Life Balance

働き方改革実現への道は遠い？

Jiji Press Photo

Key Expressions 1

CD1-34

音声を聞いて１～３の（　　）内に適当な語を書き入れましょう。

1. Japanese law (g _ _ _ _ _ _ _ _ _ _) both men and women up to one year leave from work after a child is born.
   日本の法律は、子供が生まれた後、男女ともに最長１年間まで仕事を休めることを保証している。

2. According to government data, only 6% of (e _ _ _ _ _ _ _ _) fathers take paternity leave.
   政府のデータによると、（取得の）資格がある父親のわずか6%しか育児休暇を取得していない。

3. Japan's government is now considering making parental leave (m _ _ _ _ _ _ _ _) for both men and women.
   日本政府は男女ともに対して育児休暇を義務付けることを現在考えている。

● Key Expressions 2

leave という動詞は、「出発する」「去る」「やめる」「捨てる」「休暇を取る」などの意味がありますが、「休暇を取る」という意味から派生した名詞には「休暇（期間）」という意味があります。

以下の１～５の日本語に該当する表現になるように、選択肢から適当な語を選び、（　　）内に書き入れましょう。

1. 休暇中で　(　　　　　　　　) leave
2. 産休／育休　(　　　　　　　　) leave
3. 有給休暇　(　　　　　　　　) leave
4. 介護休暇　(　　　　　　　　) leave
5. 休暇を取得する　(　　　　　　　　) a leave

take	on	paid	parental	family-care

● Key Expressions 3

人が被った被害を表す代表的な表現に受動態があります。以下の１～３は、パタハラ（男性社員が育児休業を取得する際に受ける上司・同僚からのいやがらせ）被害にあったと主張する男性の経験について述べています。（　　）内の動詞を適当な形に書き換えましょう。

1. He (sideline →　　　　　　　　) as retribution for taking his paternity leave.
彼は育児休暇を取得したことに対する報復として第一線から外された。

2. He (take →　　　　　　　　) off the career track after his paternity leave.
彼は育児休暇を取得した後、出世コースから外された。

3. He (assign →　　　　　　　　) odd tasks beyond his abilities since his second child was born.
２人目の子供が生まれてから、彼は自分の能力を超えた慣れない仕事をあてがわれている。

● Background Knowledge

育児休暇取得について、英文に述べられているものを１～４から選びましょう。

While companies in Japan are encouraged to promote parental leave and many have expressed their support for those taking time off to raise families, critics say the directives are not trickling down to employees on the ground.

Japan's government, concerned about the drastically declining birthrate—among the lowest in the world—is even considering making parental leave mandatory. In the U.S., federal laws do not guarantee paid parental leave, but many companies offer such benefits. European nations vary, but most offer some type of government-backed paid paternity leave.

The Associated Press

1. 多くの日本企業では、育児休暇を取得することが奨励されているが、その指示は現場の従業員に浸透していない。
2. 日本政府は、育児休暇取得を義務付けるのは問題であると考えている。
3. アメリカでは、法によって労働者が有給の育児休暇を取得することが保証されている。
4. ヨーロッパ各国においては、すべての労働者が有給の育児休暇を取得できる。

● Newspaper English

新聞記事では、登場人物について説明をするために、しばしば関係代名詞節が使われます。

以下の１と２の（　　）内に当てはまる適当な関係代名詞を書き入れましょう。

1. The man, (　　　　　　) sons are now four and one, took paternity leave after they were born.
現在４歳と１歳の息子がいるその男性は、彼らが生まれた後に育児休暇を取得した。

2. According to an expert, a boss is apt to think a worker (　　　　　　) takes paternity leave is useless.
ある専門家によると、上司は、育児休暇を取る男性社員は役に立たないと考えがちである。

Sportswear maker employee's lawsuit highlights paternity leave in Japan

lawsuit「訴訟」
highlight...「(問題)を浮き彫りにする」
report to...「〜の監督下にいる」
initially「当初は」
minimal「最小限の」
plaintiff「原告」
hearing「審理」
forego...「〜なしで済ませる」
name...「〜の名前を公表する」
assignment「職務」
damages「損害賠償(金)」
social studies「社会学」
go to the heart of...「〜の核心に触れる」
corporate culture「企業文化」
transfer「転勤」

TOKYO—He sits in an office of a major Japanese sportswear maker but reports to no one. The man, whose sons are now four and one, initially belonged to a sales-marketing section at the company, but now he is assigned odd tasks like translating company rules into English, though he has minimal foreign language skills.

He was sidelined, he says, as retribution for taking paternity leaves after each of his two sons was born. Now he is the plaintiff in one of the first lawsuits in Japan over "pata-hara," or paternity harassment, as it is known here. The first hearing is scheduled for this week.

His case is unusual in a country that values loyalty to the company, long hours and foregone vacations, especially from male employees. He asked not to be named for fear of further retribution.

He wants his original assignment back and 4.4 million yen ($41,000) in damages. The company said no agreement could be reached despite repeated efforts.

Makoto Yoshida, professor of social studies at Ritsumeikan University, believes acceptance of paternity leave will take decades in Japan because it goes to the heart of corporate culture, which includes not being able to refuse transfers.

"A boss is apt to think a worker who takes paternity leave is useless. The boss is likely never to have taken paternity leave himself," Yoshida said. "And once an office sees a worker getting bad treatment for taking paternity leave, no one else is going to want to do it."

Taken off the career track, the father who works at the company says he feels helpless. Still, he is proud of how he did all the cooking, cleaning and grocery shopping while he was on leave.

His lawyer said his client believes in standing up for what is right.

"He was being made an example of," the lawyer said. "This case raises the important question of whether a person must value company over family."

The Associated Press

make an example of...「～を見せしめにする」

Summary

以下の空所１～４に当てはまる語を選択肢から選び、書き入れましょう。

A male worker in a Japanese sportswear company is (1.) his employer for allegedly (2.) him after he legally took paternity leaves to help care for his two children. A social studies professor is quoted, (3.) that Japan has been slow to embrace the concept of paternity leave due to persistent beliefs about the roles of male employees, as well as a culture of fear as workers see those who do take paternity leave being punished. The case is (4.).

sidelining	suing	ongoing	arguing

● Comprehension 1

本文に登場している育児休暇を取得した男性社員に関して述べた以下の１～４を、実際に起こった順序に並べ替えましょう。

1. He took his second paternity leave.
2. His first son was born.
3. He was assigned to a sales-marketing department.
4. He spoke anonymously about his experience of being harassed.

● Comprehension 2

本文の内容に合うように、１と３の英文を完成させるのに適当なものを、２の質問の答えとして適当なものを、a～dから選びましょう。

1. The unnamed worker claims that the company has
  a. treated him unfairly because he exercised his legal rights as a worker.
  b. threatened him with being fired if he took time off for his second child.
  c. refused to assign him tasks that are suited to his expertise as a translator.
  d. ignored the ruling from a previous case he won against them.

2. According to the article, why has the man asked not to be named?
  a. He is worried about receiving further negative treatment.
  b. He still wants to protect the identity of his company.
  c. It is part of the temporary agreement he has reached.
  d. His lawyer has advised him to do so for the sake of his sons.

3. Prof. Yoshida believes acceptance of paternity leave will take a long time because
  a. workers are concerned about a potential loss in earnings.
  b. a number of today's bosses themselves have not taken paternity leave.
  c. it is difficult to find lawyers willing to take on the cases.
  d. workers have a duty to place their company before their families.

Chapter 10

For the Empowerment of Women

ある国の現状を知ることから

Roshun

Key Expressions 1

CD1-38

音声を聞いて1～3の（　　）内に適当な語を書き入れましょう。

1. A couple found that nakshi kantha embroidery could be useful for helping Bangladeshi villagers (e _ _ _) cash and improve their living conditions.
   ある夫婦は、ノクシカタという刺繍が、バングラデシュの村人たちが現金を稼ぎ、生活状態を改善するのに役に立つと考えた。

2. In 1987, they (s _ _) up a support organization called Roshun.
   1987 年に彼らはロシュンという支援組織を設立した。

3. They not only sell the products, but also organize sessions to (i _ _ _ _ _ _ _ _) nakshi kantha embroidery to Japanese consumers.
   彼らは製品を売るだけでなく、日本人消費者にノクシカタの刺繍を紹介する会を催したりもしている。

● Key Expressions 2

名詞には、-tion「動作、状態」や -ance, -ence「すること（もの）、〜な性質（状態）」を表す接尾辞がつくものがあります。

枠内の説明を参考に、以下の１〜６の動詞に適当な接尾辞をつけて名詞にしましょう。

1. allow（許可する） →[ ]（許可、手当）
2. persist（しつこく繰り返す）
→[ ]（根強さ、頑固）
3. organize（組織する） →[ ]（組織）
4. endure（耐える） →[ ]（忍耐力）
5. concentrate（集中する） →[ ]（集中）
6. accept（受け入れる） →[ ]（受容）

● Key Expressions 3

バングラデシュ製品のフェアトレードを支援する店を説明した以下の１〜３の英文の（ ）内に適当な語句を選択肢から選んで書き入れ、さらに日本語訳を完成させましょう。

1. The Roshun shop is a one-minute walk ( ) of Seibu Toritsu-Kasei Station.
ロシュンのお店は西武都立家政駅の（ ）徒歩１分のところにある。

2. It is closed on Wednesdays and may not be open ( ) when special exhibitions are held.
水曜日が定休日で、特別展示が行われる（ ）閉店している場合もある。

3. A display and sales session will take place at a gallery in Kunitachi, western Tokyo, ( ).
展示と販売は、東京の西部、国立市のギャラリーで（ ）開かれる予定である。

on days	from the south exit	from March 18 through 29

● Background Knowledge

馬上慎司さん美恵子さん夫妻の店と活動について、英文に述べられていないものを１～４から選びましょう。

The prices of cushion covers and pouches at Roshun start at 8,000 yen. Some blouses and other articles are priced at more than 50,000 yen.

When customers say that products from developing nations should be cheaper, the couple carefully explain the background, significance and exceptional quality of the items. "It moves me to tears when customers tell me that they considered our items expensive at first but then found them reasonable," Mieko said.

Although Bangladesh has recently seen rapid economic growth, many women in the important sewing industry are still forced to work in terrible conditions.

"Many challenges remain in the workplaces, but we will continue our efforts until the activity can be managed by local residents and thus be made sustainable," Mieko said.

The Asahi Shimbun

1. 彼らの店で売っているブラウスはすべて５万円以上の値がついている。
2. 新興国の製品は安くすべきだと言う客もいる。
3. バングラデシュで縫製業に就いている多くの女性たちの就業環境は悪い。
4. 二人は自分たちの活動が地元住民によって担われるようになるまで努力を続けるつもりである。

● Newspaper English

英語の文章では、同じ言い回しを何度も使用せず、同じ内容を様々に言い換えて述べられます。記事を読む時には、何がどのような表現で言い換えられているのか注意しながら読みましょう。

以下の文中の下線部を言い換えた表現として適当な語を、日本語訳を参考に１と２の英文の（　　）内に書き入れましょう。

Mieko Magami, 63, and Shinji Magami, 65, started working in Bangladesh as Japan Overseas Cooperation Volunteers in the first half of the 1980s.

1. The (　　　　　　　　) returned to Japan in 1986 and then married.
   その夫妻は 1986 年に日本に戻り、その後結婚した。
2. The (　　　　　　　　) opened the Tokyo outlet in 2003.
   馬上夫妻は 2003 年にその東京の店をオープンした。

empower...「～の自立を促す」
result in...「結果～になる」
involve...「～を巻き込む」
appeal to...「～の興味をそそる、～に訴える」
proceed with...「～を続ける」
by trial and error「試行錯誤で」
modest「控えめな」
aggressive「積極的な」

Tokyo shop deals in embroidery to empower women in Bangladesh

Mieko Magami, 63, and Shinji Magami, 65, started working in Bangladesh as Japan Overseas Cooperation Volunteers in the first half of the 1980s. They found nakshi kantha embroidery useful and saw it as a way for Bangladeshi villagers to earn cash and improve their living conditions.

But the two had to persistently ask worried husbands and fathers to allow their wives and daughters to join a training session organized in Dhaka. The effort resulted in the start of the fair trade project involving 16 members.

The couple returned to Japan in 1986 and then married. The following year, they set up a support organization called Roshun.

Shinji was working at a company in those days, but he quit his job about five years later to concentrate on the Bangladesh project.

The Magamis opened a Tokyo outlet in 2003. They have been increasingly allowed to present the products at department stores and galleries.

The couple not only sell the products but also organize sessions to introduce nakshi kantha embroidery and hold cooking lessons to help Japanese learn more about Bangladesh.

Mieko has repeatedly visited Bangladesh to work with the villagers to develop high-quality goods that would appeal to Japanese consumers.

“We proceeded with our plan by trial and error, and it required great persistence and endurance from both of us,” Mieko said.

As the project progressed, some changes arose among the villagers. Modest women began making aggressive efforts on their own, and husbands who initially opposed their spouses' working outside showed up to lend a hand.

spouse「配偶者」

Female leaders have emerged, while the number of households involved in the program has risen to 450.

The Asahi Shimbun

● Summary

以下の空所１～４に当てはまる語を選択肢から選び、書き入れましょう。

Over a number of decades, a Japanese couple has worked with people in Bangladesh to establish a fair trade (1. ______________) that sells products featuring traditional nakshi kantha (2. ______________) in Japan. The project's success has depended on a variety of factors, including the (3. ______________) of the Bangladeshi workers to embrace new roles and the Japanese couple's ongoing efforts to educate and cultivate a (4. ______________) for the artisanal products in Japan.

willingness	market	embroidery	project

● Comprehension 1

本文の内容に当てはまるように、馬上夫妻の経歴をまとめた次の年表を完成させましょう。

年	出来事
1980 年代前半	(1. 　　　　　　　　　　　　　　　　) としてバングラデシュで働き始める
1986 年	日本に (2. 　　　　　　　　　　　　　　　　)
1992 年頃	夫の慎司さんが (3. 　　　　　　　　　　　　　　　　)
2003 年	(4. 　　　　　　　　　　　　　　　　) をオープンする

● Comprehension 2

本文の内容に合うように、1と3の質問の答えとして適当なものを、2の英文を完成させるのに適当なものを、a～dから選びましょう。

1. Which of the following is one of the first challenges the couple faced?
- **a.** Finding a training venue close to the women's village
- **b.** Recruiting enough members for "fair trade" status
- **c.** The concerns of the craftswomen's male relatives
- **d.** The low manufacturing costs of the embroidery

2. Shinji Magami spent
- **a.** five years living in Japan while his wife was based in Bangladesh.
- **b.** several years working for a company while helping to run Roshun.
- **c.** many years working for a number of galleries and retailers.
- **d.** decades learning how to produce nakshi kantha embroidery himself.

3. Which of the following is NOT mentioned as a result of the project?
- **a.** The women in Bangladesh became more independent.
- **b.** The Bangladeshi men changed their attitudes about gender roles.
- **c.** Hundreds of Bangladeshi households have joined the project.
- **d.** Over 400 women have been promoted to leadership roles.

Chapter 11

Setting up Lanes for Self-Driving Cars

自動運転車、公道を走る

The Yomiuri Shimbun

● Key Expressions 1

CD2-02

音声を聞いて１～３の（　　）内に適当な語を書き入れましょう。

1. A test of trucks driving in (f_ _ _ _ _ _ _ _) is underway on the Shin-Tomei Expressway in Hamamatsu, Shizuoka Prefecture.
   静岡県浜松市の新東名高速道路で隊列走行のトラックのテスト（走行）が行われている。

2. This experiment has shown that (o _ _ _ _ _ _ _) cars coming from interchanges cannot merge smoothly into traffic because trucks drive in the leftmost lane.
   この実験では、トラックが左端の車線を走行しているので、インターチェンジから侵入する普通車が、流れにスムーズに合流できないということがわかった。

3. The test has (h _ _ _ _ _ _ _ _ _ _) the need to set up a priority lane for self-driving vehicles.
   このテスト（走行）は、自動運転車のための優先車線を設置する必要性に焦点を当てていた。

● Key Expressions 2

以下の１～６は方向を表す表現です。日本語の意味に合うように、適当な前置詞を（　　）内に書き入れましょう。複数回使うものもあります。

1. drive (　　　　　　　　) right (　　　　　　　　) left　［右から左に車を走らせる］

2. turn (　　　　　　　　) the right　［右へ曲がる］

3. keep (　　　　　　　　) the left　［左側通行］

4. the overtaking lane (　　　　　　　　) the right side　［右側の追い越し車線］

5. drive (　　　　　　　　) the leftmost lane　［左端の車線を走行する］

6. (　　　　　　　　) the right-hand lane　［右側車線沿いに］

along	to	on	in	from

● Key Expressions 3

以下の１～４は、自動運転車の現状について述べたものです。下線部の表現と日本語訳を参考に、（　　）内の動詞を適当な時制に変化させましょう。

1. Autonomous driving technology (be → 　　　　　　　　) still in the developmental stage.
自動運転技術は、まだ開発段階である。

2. So far, there (be → 　　　　　　　　) cases in which the system mistakenly identifies oncoming vehicles or cars parked on the road as obstacles, causing problems such as self-driving vehicles getting stuck on the spot.
（自動運転の）システムが、近づいてくる乗り物や路上駐車されている車を障害物と誤って認識し、自動運転車がその場で立ち往生するというような問題が、これまでに起きている。

3. At the end of last August, a golf cart-type self-driving vehicle (have → 　　　　　　　　) a minor collision with an ordinary car in Toyota, Aichi prefecture.
昨年の８月末、愛知県豊田市で、ゴルフカート型の自動運転車が普通車と軽く衝突した。

4. The Land, Infrastructure, Transport and Tourism Ministry hopes that the establishment of priority lanes (help → 　　　　　　　　) prevent accidents.
国土交通省は、優先車線の設置が事故防止に役立つだろうと期待している。

● Background Knowledge

自動運転の国際基準について、英文に述べられていないものを１～４から選びましょう。

The international standard for automated driving has six levels, from Level 0, in which the driver performs all operations, to Level 5, in which the self-driving system handles everything. Under Level 3, the self-driving system will operate instead of the driver under certain conditions, such as on expressways. The Japanese government has set a goal to put Level 3 into practical use.

The Japan News

1. レベル０では、運転者がすべての運転操作を行う。
2. レベル３では、運転者がある条件下で自動走行を行う。
3. レベル５では、運転が完全に自動化される。
4. 日本政府は、レベル３の自動走行をすでに認可している。

● Newspaper English

ニュース記事には、表やグラフや図版などの視覚情報が添えられていることがあります。これらは、記事内容をより正確に理解する手助けになります。

図版の１と２に入るものとして適当なものをａ～ｄから選びましょう。

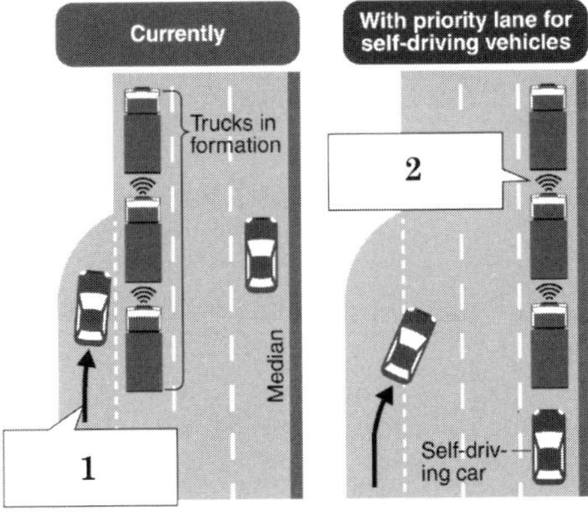

The Yomiuri Shimbun

a. ordinary vehicles can have difficulty merging smoothly
b. autonomous vehicles cannot pass ordinary ones
c. merging lane reserved for vehicles in formation
d. priority lane for autonomous vehicles

legal revision「法改正」
eye...「～を検討する」
submit a bill「法案を提出する」
relevant「関連の」
ordinary Diet session「通常国会」
provision「条項」
convert... to ～「…を～に変更する」
National Police Agency「警察庁」
authorities「関係当局」
traffic congestion「交通渋滞」
distribution「配送」
prompt...「～を促す」
artery「幹線道路」

Legal revisions eyed to set up priority lanes for automated driving

The Land, Infrastructure, Transport and Tourism Ministry plans to set up priority lanes for self-driving vehicles on some sections of expressways and other general roads, The Yomiuri Shimbun has learned.

Establishing such sections is aimed at preventing accidents and achieving smoother operation of automated driving by separating its lanes from those of ordinary vehicles. The ministry plans to submit a bill to revise relevant laws to next year's ordinary Diet session at the earliest. The bill will include provisions for setting up exclusive access roads to expressways and burying electric wires that guide self-driving vehicles under roads.

The first such lane on an expressway is expected to be set up on a section in Shizuoka Prefecture of the Shin-Tomei Expressway. The section will gradually be widened to three lanes in fiscal 2020 or later. The overtaking lane on the right side will be converted to a lane only for autonomous vehicles.

The ministry will hold discussions with the National Police Agency, among other authorities, to decide the details of the system, including how to use the lane in times of traffic congestion.

The government has set a goal to put "Level 3" of the international standard for autonomous driving into practical use as early as 2020, mainly on expressways where technical hurdles are relatively low chiefly because there are no traffic lights.

Due to labor shortages, there is expected to be more distribution via trucks driving in formation, prompting the ministry to increase the number of priority lanes on multilane highways that serve as main arteries.

On ordinary roads, the ministry plans to set up special sections where only self-driving cars can operate, mainly in sparsely populated areas with little traffic. Roads with such sections must not have houses or shops along the street, and there must be a detour for ordinary cars to pass through. The ministry will discuss with the NPA ways to warn drivers of ordinary cars not to enter such sections.

The Japan News

sparsely populated「人口密度が低い」

detour「迂回路」

● Summary

CD2-05

以下の空所１～４に当てはまる語を選択肢から選び、書き入れましょう。

With the growing prospect of various levels of autonomous (1.) on the nation's roads, Japan's government and other (2.) are working on new laws and provisions to help traditional and self-driving cars coexist on the same roads. Changes include dedicated lanes for autonomous cars and trucks on (3.) and even complete (4.) of some other types of road.

vehicles	highways	authorities	sections

● Comprehension 1

以下の１～４は文脈によって色々な意味を持つ単語です。本文中で使われている意味を a ～ d から選びましょう。

1. lane　(　　)
2. artery　(　　)
3. hurdle　(　　)
4. provision　(　　)

a. an important road
b. one of the parts that a wide road or highway is divided into
c. a part of a law that deals with a particular issue
d. a problem that you need to overcome to achieve something

● Comprehension 2

本文の内容に合うように、１と３の英文を完成させるのに適当なものを、２の質問の答えとして適当なものを、a ～ d から選びましょう。

1. At the time the article was originally written, the Land, Infrastructure, Transport and Tourism Ministry had
a. successfully trialled an exclusive highway lane for self-driving cars.
b. issued the manufacturers of autonomous vehicles with a large bill.
c. decided to submit several ideas for consideration to the government.
d. reported that there were too many accidents involving self-driving cars.

2. Which of the following has NOT been decided yet?
a. Where the first autonomous vehicle-only highway lane will be
b. Which side of the road the self-driving lane will be put on
c. The earliest date by which the highway in Shizuoka will be widened
d. What the policies for self-driving cars will be during traffic jams

3. The main reason why it is easier to adapt highways than other roads is because
a. there is relatively little traffic on Japan's highways.
b. cars are not usually required to stop on highways.
c. there are not enough workers available to do all the roads.
d. the National Police Agency has complete control of the highways.

Chapter 12

High School Hawker Scaring Away Nuisance Birds

高校生鷹匠、タカとともに生きる

The Asahi Shimbun

● Key Expressions 1

CD2-06

音声を聞いて1～3の（　　）内に適当な語を書き入れましょう。

1. Pigeons are known to carry bacteria and viruses, and their droppings present serious (h _ _ _ _ _ _) problems.
   ハトはバクテリアやウイルスを持っていることが知られており、そのふんは深刻な衛生上の問題となる。

2. A father and son are (a _ _ _ _ _ _ _) to take the family business to new heights.
   ある父子が家族経営の事業を新たな高みに押し上げることを目指している。

3. Taking over his father's work for the day, the son (r _ _ _ _ _ _ _) a Harris's hawk.
   父親からその日の仕事を引き継ぐと、息子は一羽のハリスホークを放った。

● Key Expressions 2

英語では、同じ語が名詞としても動詞としても用いられることがよくあります。名詞・動詞それぞれの意味をおさえて、語彙力を増強しましょう。

以下の１～５の意味をもつ「名詞から派生した動詞」を選択肢から選び、（　　）内に書き入れましょう。

1. ～を収容する、～に場所を提供する　（　　　　　　　　）
2. ～を悩ませる　（　　　　　　　　）
3. ～の周りを旋回する　（　　　　　　　　）
4. ～に直面する　（　　　　　　　　）
5. ～に名前をつける　（　　　　　　　　）

plague	name	house	circle	face

● Key Expressions 3

日本語訳を参考に、以下の１～４の（　　）中に当てはまる語句を選択肢から選び、書き入れましょう。

1. The presence of a hawk keeps the pigeons (　　　　　　　　).
タカの存在がハトを寄せつけない。

2. The young hawker said to his instructor, "Thank you for your advice. I'll keep it (　　　　　　　　)."
「ご忠告ありがとうございます。肝に銘じます」とその若き鷹匠は師匠に言った。

3. The high school hawker always keeps his hawking equipment (　　　　　　　　).
その高校生鷹匠はいつも自分の鷹匠としての装備をすぐ近くに置いている。

4. "Bird droppings are unhygienic. Keep them (　　　　　　　　) reach of children."
「鳥のふんは非衛生的です。子どもたちの手が届かないようにしておいてください」。

at hand	out of	in mind	at bay

● Background Knowledge

小川伸一さんがタカによる害鳥対策の事業を始めた当時の出来事について、英文に述べられているものを1～4から選びましょう。

Influenced by his son, Shinichi Ogawa also started rearing a hawk. "I was envious of the trusting relationship that my son and the hawk were building," he said.

The Ogawa family set up a home for hawks at their house in Shinto village. They trained the hawks to feel safe by walking around the area with one resting on the left arm. The business opportunity was born out of problems faced by neighbors, with pigeon droppings being left on cow enclosures and other areas. When the Ogawas released a hawk, other birds dived for cover.

The Asahi Shimbun

Notes cow enclosure「牛舎」 dive for cover「逃げるために急下降する」

1. 父親とタカとの信頼関係を羨ましく思い、伸一さんの息子もタカを飼い始めた。

2. 榛東(しんとう)村の自宅にタカのための小屋を設営し、タカを安心させるよう調教した。

3. 小川さんのタカが近隣の牛舎周辺にふんをして、近所の人々に迷惑をかけてしまった。

4. 小川さん親子がタカを放つと他の鳥たちは逃げていったが、すぐに舞い戻ってきた。

● Newspaper English

英語では、24-hour operation（24時間営業）などのように、数値と単位をハイフンでつないで形容詞として用いることがよくあります。このとき数量単位は常に単数形になります。

日本語訳を参考にして、以下の1と2の（　）中に当てはまる語を、書き入れましょう。

1. The young hawker took a (　　　　　　　　) bus ride to the building in Numata city.
若き鷹匠は40分間バスに乗り、沼田市にあるその建物に行った。

2. The (　　　　　　　　) Terrace Numata building houses the Numata city office and various restaurants.
7階建てのテラス沼田には沼田市役所やさまざまなレストランが入っている。

● Reading

Finding success in getting hawks to do what comes naturally to them

Shinichi Ogawa, 48, runs a service to discourage birds from encroaching and leaving droppings on buildings and other sites by releasing a hawk to circle overhead. His son, Ryosuke, has been helping out since October.

On a day in late November, Ryosuke arrived at a job site after school and changed into his work uniform, saying enthusiastically: “Let’s get started! I’m busy and have responsibilities, but this work is fulfilling.” The third-year Oze High School student had taken a 40-minute bus ride to the seven-story Terrace Numata building that houses the Numata city office and various restaurants.

Taking over his father’s work for the day, Ryosuke released a Harris’s hawk named Luke from the rooftop. The presence of a hawk, a natural predator, keeps the pigeons at bay.

Terrace Numata had been plagued by pigeon droppings since it opened in May. Pigeons tend to gravitate toward open ceilings and handrails, and floors in the building have been covered with the bird feces. The city office set up protective nets covering about 1,300 square meters, but was unable to solve the problem. Eventually, city officials asked the Ogawa family to help out. Since this autumn, a hawk has regularly patrolled the skies above the building and pigeon droppings have decreased.

Ryosuke, one of a few high school student hawkers in Japan, loves birds and has aspired to become a hawker since seeing one on TV when he was a sixth-grader in elementary school. He encountered a Harris’s hawk and met an instructor at a specialized raptor shop in Ushiku, Ibaraki Prefecture. He has since been taking training sessions there and had won the Harris’s hawk section of Flight Festa, one of the biggest raptor competitions in Japan, three years in a

come naturally to…「～にとって簡単である」
encroach on…「～を侵害する」
overhead「頭上で（に）」
enthusiastically「熱心に」
fulfilling「充実して」
Harris’s hawk「モモアカノスリ（和名）：タカの一種、ハリスホーク（英名）と呼ばれることが多い」
natural predator「天敵」
gravitate toward…「～に引き寄せられる」
open ceiling「吹き抜け」
feces「ふん、排せつ物」
eventually「最終的に、たまりかねて」
encounter…「～に出会う」
raptor「猛禽（類）」
in a row「連続して」

row. He plans to improve his hawking skills away from home after graduating from high school, in the hope of joining his dad full-time.

Their business clients, mainly local companies, range from large commercial facilities in the greater Tokyo area and leading automakers to factories and warehouses of transportation firms. With the number of contracts doubling compared with last year, the Ogawas now have six hawks.

The Asahi Shimbun

commercial facility「商業施設」
transportation firm「運送会社」
contract「契約」

● Summary

以下の空所１～４に当てはまる語を選択肢から選び、書き入れましょう。

A father and son team have turned their love of hawking into a viable enterprise, hiring out their (1.) and hawks to local businesses who want to reduce the numbers of nuisance (2.) around their buildings. Their (3.) include commercial businesses and local governments. The son, a high school student, has won (4.) with his birds, and hopes to join his father full-time after graduating from high school.

skills	prizes	clients	birds

● Comprehension 1

テラス沼田について、本文の内容に当てはまるものには T（True）を、当てはまらないものには F（False）を（　）内に書き入れましょう。

1. Its roof has been covered with bird feces. (　　)

2. It takes 40 minutes by bus from the Numata city office to get there. (　　)

3. There are various restaurants in it. (　　)

4. The city office set up protective nets there before it asked the Ogawas to help. (　　)

● Comprehension 2

本文の内容に合うように、1と3の英文を完成させるのに適当なものを、2の質問の答えとして適当なものを、a～d から選びましょう。

1. Ryosuke Ogawa arrived at Terrace Numata

a. already wearing his uniform.

b. in his father's work van.

c. after completing a day at school.

d. feeling unhappy about his work.

2. Why did the city office contact the Ogawas?

a. To rescue an injured pigeon that had flown into the net

b. To clean up the droppings left by over one thousand birds

c. To come and relocate a lost hawk that was living on the roof

d. To deter pigeons after previous strategies proved unsuccessful

3. Ryosuke first learned about hawking after

a. seeing a hawker in the media.

b. visiting a shop in Ibaraki.

c. accompanying his dad to work.

d. attending Flight Festa as a child.

Chapter 13

Fusion of AI with Human Sensibility

AIの弟子を持つデザイナー

The Yomiuri Shimbun

● Key Expressions 1

CD2-10

写真に関する音声を聞いて１～３の（　　）内に適当な語を書き入れましょう。

1. EMarie specializes in bridal wear aiming to (m _ _ _ _ _ _ _) the beauty of each woman on her special day.
エマリーエは、一人一人の女性の美をその人の特別な日に最大限引き出すことを目指したブライダル衣装を専門としている。

2. The dress on the right was designed by Ema Rie based on an output by AI that (a _ _ _ _ _ _ _) about 1,000 images of roses.
右のドレスは、およそ 1,000 のバラの画像を分析した AI によるアウトプットをもとに、エマ理永さんがデザインした。

3. The idea that humans and AI can (c _ _ _ _ _ _ _ _) is fascinating.
人間と AI が協力できるという考えは興味深い。

● Key Expressions 2

-ity は、形容詞から抽象名詞を作る接尾辞で、元の形容詞の示す性質や状態を表します。接合部の綴りが変わるものもありますので注意しましょう。

以下の1～5の形容詞をもとにして名詞を作りましょう。

1. uniform（均一の、画一の） → [ ]（均一性、画一性）
2. diverse（多様な） → [ ]（多様性）
3. complex（複雑な） → [ ]（複雑さ）
4. objective（客観的な） → [ ]（客観性）
5. creative（独創的な） → [ ]（独創性）

● Key Expressions 3

〈make ＋目的語＋補語〉の構文では、補語に目的語を説明する語句が置かれ、「目的語を～の状態にする」という意味を表します。日本語訳を参考に、以下の1～4の英文の［ ］内の語句を正しく並べ替えましょう。

1. The idea of collaborating [excited / made / with / the designer / AI technology].
AI 技術とコラボするという考えが、そのデザイナーをわくわくさせた。

____

2. The designer's goal is to [happy / women / by creating / make / clothes] that perfectly fit their bodies.
そのデザイナーの目標は、体にぴったり合う服を作り出すことによって、女性たちを幸せにすることである。

____

3. AI technology can [more / the fashion / make / sustainable / industry].
AI 技術はファッション業界をより持続可能なものにすることができる。

____

4. More advanced technology could usher in an age of haute couture by [individually created / more / clothes / making / affordable].
より先端の技術は、個人用に作られた服をより手の届く価格にすることによって、オートクチュールの時代を導くことが可能となるだろう。

____

● Background Knowledge

2005年以降のエマ理永さんの活躍について、英文に述べられていないものを1～4から選びましょう。

In 2005, Ema Rie's realm of fashion expanded into space when she presided over a Space Couture Design Contest as part of a Japan Aerospace Exploration Agency (JAXA) project. She created a buzz at home and abroad when she designed a dress for the world's first wedding held in zero gravity, which was covered by major newspapers such as *The New York Times* and *The Guardian*. Her name has also been mentioned in leading scientific journal *Nature* for her unconventional approach.

The Japan News

Notes realm「領域」 unconventional「型にはまらない」

1. スペース・クチュール・デザインコンテストの委員長を務めた。
2. 世界初の無重力空間で行われた結婚式のためにドレスをデザインした。
3. ニューヨークタイムズ紙などで取り上げられ、国内外で話題となった。
4. ネイチャー誌にファッションとAIに関する論文を発表した。

● Newspaper English

kimonoやsushiなど、ある言語でもそのまま使われるようになった外国語の単語を借用語といいます。ファッションの分野ではフランス語からの借用語が多いので、発音にも注意してぜひ覚えておきましょう。

日本語訳を参考に、以下の1～3の英文の（　　）内に当てはまる語句を選択肢から選び、書き入れましょう。

1. Ema's career in ( ) is at 30 years and counting.
   エマさんのオート・クチュールにおけるキャリアは30年以上である。
2. This type of skirt with a feminine ( ) is very popular now.
   女性的なシルエットのこのタイプのスカートは、今とても人気がある。
3. A designer opened a chic ( ) selling clothes designed by AI.
   あるデザイナーはAIによってデザインされた服を売るしゃれたブティックをオープンした。

boutique	silhouette	haute couture

maverick「型破りな、非正統的な」
fuse「融合する」
superb「最高の、すばらしい」
apprentice「弟子」
eager to...「～したがる」
a wide range of...「幅広い～」
fine arts「美術」
urge...「(人に～するよう強く)促す」
potential「潜在的能力」
garment「衣服」
ready-made「既製の」
conform to...「～に合う」
elevate...「～を高める」
lag behind「遅れをとる」
mass production「大量生産」
benefit「利益」
showcase...「～を披露する、～を見せる」
venue「会場」
sway「揺れる」
evoke...「～を想起させる」

'Maverick' designer fuses fashion with science

For wedding dress designer Ema Rie, artificial intelligence is like a "superb apprentice." Her apprentice is eager to learn once a task is given, and presents a wide range of designs to her, some of which are beyond her imagination.

Her career in haute couture is at 30 years and counting. Initially, however, fashion was the last thing Ema had in mind for her career. She studied fine arts at a high school in Aichi Prefecture, and craft design at a junior college in Tokyo. The turning point came in the 1980s after she moved to Chicago with her husband. She intended to go to a local college to improve her English, but her American friends urged her to study fashion as they saw her potential. After entering a fashion design course at college, she won one contest, then another.

Her goal is to make women happy by creating clothes that perfectly fit their bodies. She believes such garments—rather than ready-made products to which people must conform—can maximize the individual beauty of each person. She says advanced technology holds the key to elevating fashion from uniformity to diversity.

"The fashion world has lagged behind in introducing technology." Ema said. "Mass production has delivered significant benefits, but more advanced technology could usher in an age of haute couture by making individually created clothes more affordable."

In late November, "collaborative works" produced by Ema and AI technology were showcased in Yokohama at a venue that seemed out of place for a fashion show: a symposium hosted by Riken, one of the nation's largest research institutes. As hip-hop music played, models wearing dresses created jointly by Ema and AI walked down the runway. When the models walked, the dresses swayed, evoking beautiful feminine silhouettes.

A team of Riken researchers used AI to analyze about 500 of Ema's works along with images of objects such as shells and roses, and then output designs. Ema then used the designs as inspiration to bring dresses to life for the show. At the symposium, a red and white dress in a flamboyant rose design drew particular attention, with many in the audience taking photos.

The Japan News

bring...to life「〜を生み出す」
flamboyant「きらびやかな、大胆な」
draw attention「注目を集める」

● Summary

以下の空所１～４に当てはまる語を選択肢から選び、書き入れましょう。

An (1. ______________________) Japanese fashion designer, Ema Rie, has embraced artificial intelligence (AI) in order to revolutionize her design process. Collaborating with researchers, the designer presented the results of their work at a (2. ______________________) show. The designer believes that, despite what she sees as the fashion industry's (3. ______________________) adoption of AI, the technology has the potential to make (4. ______________________) clothing more affordable.

slow	American-trained	bespoke	runway

● Comprehension 1

以下の１～４の出来事が起こった場所を選択肢から選び、(　　) 内に書き入れましょう。

1. Ema entered a fashion design course at a local college.
(　　　　　　　　　　　　)

2. Ema studied fine arts at a high school. (　　　　　　　　　　　　)

3. Collaborative works produced by Ema and AI technology were showcased.
(　　　　　　　　　　　　)

4. She studied craft design at a junior college. (　　　　　　　　　　　　)

Yokohama	Chicago	Tokyo	Aichi

● Comprehension 2

本文の内容に合うように、１～３の英文を完成させるのに適当なものをａ～ｄから選びましょう。

1. Ema Rie was

a. highly praised for the designs she produced during an apprenticeship.
b. encouraged to improve her English before entering the fashion industry.
c. interested in careers other than fashion before she moved to the United States.
d. reluctant to move to the United States after she got married.

2. Ema Rie believes that

a. AI is useful for mass-produced clothing, but unsuitable for haute couture.
b. people should work hard to make their bodies the ideal size.
c. high prices are an important part of haute couture's charm.
d. women look their best when their clothing fits them perfectly.

3. Riken researchers

a. advised Ema Rie on how to minimize waste in the manufacturing process.
b. helped the AI learn about Ema's aesthetic by letting it analyze past designs.
c. helped Ema to embroider around 500 rose designs on one particular dress.
d. have used AI to create a new material for buttons from sea shells.

Chapter 14

Infrastructure Inspection Using Drones

老朽化する日本のインフラを守れ！

The Yomiuri Shimbun

● Key Expressions 1

CD2-14

写真に関する音声を聞いて１～３の（　　）内に適当な語を書き入れましょう。

1. Bridges (c _ _ _ _ _ _ _ _ _ _ _) 50 years ago or earlier are considered aging.
   50 年以上前に建設された橋は、老朽化していると見なされる。

2. In the above picture, a drone takes a video of a noise (b _ _ _ _ _ _) at a point 50 meters above the ground.
   上の写真では、ドローンが地上50メートル地点で遮音壁のビデオを撮影している。

3. The introduction of drones has (d _ _ _ _ _ _ _ _ _ _ _) changed the way the inspections are done.
   ドローンの導入は点検の仕方を劇的に変えた。

● Key Expressions 2

以下の１～６はインフラの整備・保全に関する語です。日本語訳を選択肢から選び、（　）内に書き入れましょう。

1. collapse　（　　　　　　　　）
2. adhesive　（　　　　　　　　）
3. degradation　（　　　　　　　　）
4. corrosion　（　　　　　　　　）
5. cracking　（　　　　　　　　）
6. defect　（　　　　　　　　）

亀裂・ひび	欠陥	腐食	倒壊・崩落	劣化	接着剤

● Key Expressions 3

「in... of 形式」の熟語は種類が多いだけでなく、意味範囲も広く、さまざまな場面で頻繁に用いられます。日本語訳を参考に、以下の１～４の英文の［　］内の語句を正しく並べ替えましょう。

1. High-strength fiber [in / used / place / is / of] steel reinforcement bars in this new concrete.
   この新しいコンクリートには、鉄筋の代わりに高強度繊維が使われている。

   ____

2. In this region, roughly 80% of the bridges [are / repairs / of / in / need].
   この地域では、橋のおよそ 80% は修理の必要がある。

   ____

3. The man over there is [charge / the new drone / of / in / development] project.
   あちらの男性は新型ドローン開発プロジェクトの責任者です。

   ____

4. Most people are [idea / of / the / favor / in] of preventive maintenance.
   ほとんどの人々が予防保全という考えに賛成である。

   ____

● Background Knowledge

日本のインフラ保守・整備にかかる費用について、英文に述べられているものを１～４から選びましょう。

According to an estimate by the transport ministry, the costs associated with maintaining and improving Japan's infrastructure had climbed to approximately ¥5.2 trillion a year as of fiscal 2018.

Taking a "corrective maintenance" approach, doing repairs on facilities only after issues such as cracking or corrosion emerge, would result in those costs surpassing the ¥10 trillion mark in fiscal 2048. On the other hand, taking a preventive maintenance approach, performing repair work before problems occur, would limit costs to an approximate maximum of ¥6.5 trillion within the same time frame.

The Japan News

1. 国土交通省はインフラの保守・整備にかかる費用が、2018年度の時点でおよそ5兆2千億円に上ると試算した。
2. 予防保全の場合は、インフラの保守・整備費用は2048年度で10兆円を超えるだろう。
3. 事後保全の場合は、2048年度におけるインフラの保守・整備費用は6兆5千億円までに抑えられるだろう。
4. 予防保全でも事後保全でも、およそ30年後のインフラの保守・整備費用はあまり変わらない。

● Newspaper English

語尾が -ing 形の語は、動名詞か現在分詞のどちらかであるのが普通です。しかし、following（～の後に）、regarding（～に関して）、considering（～を考慮すれば）のように、前置詞としての働きを持つものもあります。英文記事でもよく使われますので、ぜひ覚えておきましょう。

日本語訳を参考に、以下の１と２の（　　）内に入る適当な語を選択肢から選び、書き入れましょう。

1. The company turned to drones ( ) the accident in 2012.
   その企業は2012年の事故の後、ドローンに目を向けた。
2. Please contact me if you have any questions ( ) the inspection next week.
   来週の点検に関して何かご質問がございましたら、私にご連絡ください。

regarding	following

Reading

Drones recruited to inspect aging bridges, roads

In August 2019, it was revealed that among roughly 770,000 assets such as bridges and tunnels in locations across the country, approximately 80,000—or about 10%—have been assessed as requiring repairs within the next five years.

"Right, right ... Now a little to the left," a worker in a helmet was calling out instructions while checking a monitor under a bridge on the Ken-o Expressway that crosses the Sagami River in Sagamihara, Kanagawa Prefecture, in early December 2019.

Displayed on the screen was an anchor bolt, which was holding in place a noise barrier located 50 meters above the ground. Circling overhead, a camera-equipped drone was taking a series of snapshots, allowing the workers to make sure the bolt had not come loose, and to check for other defects.

Inspections of this nature would once be performed by eye, by workers standing on elevating platforms or suspended from ropes. The introduction of drones has drastically changed the way these inspections are done.

The highway is managed by the Central Nippon Expressway Co. Group, which began developing drones for inspection purposes in fiscal 2014.

The company turned to drones following the collapse of concrete ceiling panels in the Sasago Tunnel on the Chuo Expressway in 2012. The accident occurred when the anchor bolts that supported the ceiling panels gave way due to factors including the degradation of adhesives.

Many roads, bridges, and other infrastructure assets around Japan were built during the high-growth era of the 1960s and 1970s. Concrete is generally expected to show signs of degradation, such as corrosion and cracking, by its 50th year in service.

assets「資産」
assess...「〜を判定する、〜を査定する」
call out...「〜を大声で言う」
anchor bolt「アンカーボルト」
hold... in place「〜を固定する」
come loose「緩む」
elevating platform「高所作業車」
suspend...「〜を吊り下げる」
give way「抜け落ちる、崩れる」
the high-growth era「高度成長時代」
in service「使用されて」

With the aim of doubling that life expectancy to upward of 100 years, Taisei Corp. has developed a concrete in which high-strength fiber is used in place of steel reinforcement bars. According to the company, this concrete offers the benefits of high density and reduced permeability, and is less susceptible to being penetrated by water and salt, which cause cracking and corrosion. Technological innovation may prove to be a secret weapon in municipalities' efforts to formulate strategies for dealing with aging infrastructure.

The Japan News

life expectancy「寿命」
upward of...「～を超える」
density「密度」
permeability「透過性」
susceptible to...「～の影響を受けやすい」
penetrate...「～にしみ込む」
prove to be...「～であることがわかる」
municipality「地方自治体」
formulate...「～を策定する」

Summary

CD2-17

以下の空所１～４に当てはまる語句を選択肢から選び、書き入れましょう。

Around one tenth of Japan's (1.) infrastructure, including bridges and tunnels, is expected to need structural repairs within the (2.) five years. Various companies are investing in technology in order to carry out difficult inspections and increase the performance of building materials. These innovations include developing new forms of more (3.) concrete and using (4.) drones to make the assessment of such infrastructure easier.

next	aging	camera-equipped	durable

● Comprehension 1

以下の１～４の出来事を、実際に起こった順序に並べ替えましょう。

1. The workers inspected a bridge over the Sagami River using a drone.
2. The Central Nippon Expressway Co. Group began developing drones for inspection purposes.
3. It was revealed that about 10 percent of all the infrastructure assets in Japan will need repairs within five years.
4. The concrete ceiling panels in the Sasago Tunnel collapsed.

(　　　) → (　　　) → (　　　) → (　　　)

● Comprehension 2

本文の内容に合うように、１と３の英文を完成させるのに適当なものを、２の質問の答えとして適当なものを、a～dから選びましょう。

1. At least one of the people working on the Ken-o Expressway was
a. carrying out repairs on the monitor.
b. taking photos while hanging from a rope.
c. wearing protective headgear.
d. shielding his coworkers from the noise.

2. When did Central Nippon Expressway Co. Group start to invest in drones?
a. After a serious accident was caused by structural degradation
b. Before an accident occurred in the tunnel on the Chuo Expressway
c. While the government encouraged it to do so
d. When the price of drones was much less

3. Concrete using high-strength fibers is superior to that containing steel reinforcement bars because it
a. contains less salt originally.
b. produces more salt over time.
c. is more resistant to salt.
d. has a higher salt to water ratio.

Chapter 15

Use Your Aesthetics in Business

アートが突破口！？

The National Museum of Modern Art, Tokyo

● Key Expressions 1

CD2-18

音声を聞いて１～３の（　　）内に適当な語を書き入れましょう。

1. Seminars on fine art (a _ _ _ _ _ _ _ _ _ _ _ _) and interactive courses at art museums are becoming popular.
美術館での美術鑑賞セミナーやインタラクティブコースが人気となってきている。

2. These seminars train people's ability to generate ideas by refining their artistic sensibilities and then show them how to use this ability to make (b _ _ _ _ _ _ _ _ _ _ _ _) in business settings.
これらのセミナーは、人々の芸術的感受性を磨くことでアイデアを生み出す能力を訓練し、そしてビジネスの現場で突破口を開くためにこの能力をどう使うのかを人々に示す。

3. The participants are not allowed to (d _ _ _) each other's opinions under the seminar's rules.
このセミナーのルールでは、参加者たちはお互いの意見を否定することを許されていない。

● Key Expressions 2

動詞 make を使った熟語はたくさんあり、できるだけ多く覚えておくと便利です。日本語訳を参考に、1～6の（　　）内に適当な語を選択肢より選び、書き入れましょう。

1. make the (　　　　　　) of...　[～を最大限に利用する]
2. make (　　　　　　) of...　[～を利用する]
3. make (　　　　　　) for...　[～の埋め合わせをする]
4. make (　　　　　　) of...　[～をからかう]
5. make (　　　　　　) of...　[～を軽視する]
6. make up one's (　　　　　　)　[決心する]

up	mind	fun	most	light	use

● Key Expressions 3

日本語訳を参考に、以下の1～3の英文の（　　）内に適当な熟語を選択肢より選び、書き入れましょう。

1. Universities also (　　　　　　) how art and design can be applied to business and society.
   大学もアートとデザインをビジネスや社会にどのように応用できるかに注意を向けている。

2. In producing designs, it is essential to (　　　　　　) what society needs and to (　　　　　　) of users.
   デザインを生む際に、社会が何を必要としているか考え、ユーザーの立場になってみることが不可欠である。

3. "I presume that if the way of thinking in designs is tactfully incorporated into the economy, perhaps it will be possible to (　　　　　　) stagnation," said Masanori Aoyagi, the chairman of the board of directors of Tama Art University in Setagaya Ward, Tokyo.
   「デザインの考え方を上手く経済に取り入れられれば、不況を抜け出すことができるかもしれないと思います」と東京の世田谷区にある、学校法人多摩美術大学理事長の青柳正規氏は述べた。

break free from	figure out	put oneself in the shoes	pay attention to

● Background Knowledge

横浜美術館について、英文に述べられていないものを１～４から選びましょう。

The Yokohama Museum of Art supports in-house training programs of companies in the neighborhood and makes original curricula tailored to the companies' requests. One such company in Yokohama carried out an educational program for employees involved in a new project in collaboration with the museum. Five kilograms of clay were given to each of the employees, who were divided into teams in order to create a town model using the clay. As they exchanged opinions and deepened mutual understanding, they were reportedly able to start the project smoothly.

The Japan News

1. 近隣の企業に社内研修プログラムの支援を行っている。
2. 企業のリクエストに応じた研修カリキュムを提供している。
3. 横浜市のある企業向けの研修を美術館で行った。
4. その研修では粘土を使って町のモデルを作りながら意見交換をして相互理解を深めた。

● Newspaper English

サービスや行事・イベントの内容を紹介する新聞記事の場合、それらの行われる場所、時間、価格などの詳細情報が盛り込まれます。

日本語訳を参考に、以下の１～３の（　　）内に当てはまる動詞を選び、必要なら形を変えて書き入れましょう。

The museum holds three seminars a year under the program. Each seminar (1. 　　　　　　) about 3½ hours and (2. 　　　　　　) ¥20,000 per person, yet they are so popular that the 30 spots always (3. 　　　　　　) up quickly.

その美術館ではこのプログラムで年間３回のセミナーを開催する。各セミナーの時間は約３時間半で、一人２万円だが、非常に人気があるため 30 名の定員は常にすぐに満席となる。

fill	last	cost

thrive「繁栄する」
prove...「～であるとわかる」
foster...「～を育成する」
human resources「人材」
nurture...「～を育成する」
cultural property「文化財」
represent...「～を代表する」
individuality「個性」
face to face「面と向かって」

Study art to thrive in business: Art museums, universities offer programs for adults, companies

There is a growing trend of learning art and design and making the most of it in business. Seminars on fine art appreciation and interactive courses at art museums are proving very popular, while some universities are holding open courses on fostering human resources with an emphasis on art.

These are all attempts at training people's ability to generate ideas by refining their artistic sensibility and then showing them how to use this ability to make breakthroughs in business settings.

"What do you feel when you look at this work?" asked a staff member at the National Museum of Modern Art, Tokyo, during the seminar "Dialogue in the Museum" on Jan. 25. The participants gave various responses, such as, "She has strong facial features," "Looks like she's lying down watching TV," and "Maybe the artist wanted to paint a powerful woman."

The educational program started in June last year to nurture people's abilities to think and make accurate observations in business settings by becoming aware of something new through viewing and discussing works of art at the museum in Chiyoda Ward, Tokyo.

The aforementioned opinions were given in response to one of the works discussed on that day: "Ratai Bijin" (Nude Beauty), a famous oil painting by Tetsugoro Yorozu (1885–1927). Designated as an important cultural property, it represents an era when Japanese society began appreciating individuality in art.

Yet such background information was not given to the participants as they stood face to face in front of the artworks. And under the seminar's rules, they were not allowed to deny each other's opinions.

"There's no correct answer to what you see when you look at a painting. I hope people will interpret works of art without any preconceptions," said curator Akiko Ichijo of the museum's program development department in charge of the seminar series.

preconception「先入観」

The seminar that day ended with a lecture by writer Shu Yamaguchi, whose books include "Sekai no Elite wa naze Biishiki wo Kitaerunoka?" (Why do the world's elite train their aesthetics?).

"I'd like to make good use of what I learned today in my job, which is related to human resources development," said a 45-year-old company employee who participated in the event.

The Japan News

Summary

CD2-21

以下の空所１～４に当てはまる語を選択肢から選び、書き入れましょう。

A number of institutions involved in art curation and art education are offering (1.   ) programs to clients from outside the (2.   ) world. The idea is that by learning how to appreciate artistic works, clients will develop skills that are transferable to their (3.   ) roles, such as observation, keeping an (4.   ) mind and listening to the opinions of others.

art	corporate	training	open

● Comprehension 1

本文に述べられている東京国立近代美術館のセミナーの参加者ができるようになると思われることを、以下の1～5からすべて選びましょう。

1. To become good at painting
2. To become aware of new things in daily life
3. To observe things accurately
4. To improve skills in appreciating fine arts
5. To learn how to become art buyers

● Comprehension 2

本文の内容に合うように、1と3の質問の答えとして適当なものを、2の英文を完成させるのに適当なものを、a～dから選びましょう。

1. According to the article, which of the following things did participants in the January 25 seminar NOT comment on?
  a. The honesty of the person in the painting
  b. The appearance of the woman in the picture
  c. The posture of the female figure depicted in the work
  d. The intention behind the artist's choice of subject

2. One of the reasons "Ratai Bijin" is notable is because
  a. it was painted by several individuals.
  b. its importance has been officially recognized.
  c. it was the first oil painting by a Japanese artist.
  d. it was missing for over forty years.

3. Which of the following best describes the opinion of the company employee quoted at the end of the article?
  a. They hope to apply some of the ideas they encountered to their daily work.
  b. They found it difficult to make a link between art and human resources.
  c. They have been a fan of Shu Yamaguchi's books for some time.
  d. They think the human resources department of the museum is very good.

Chapter 16

Tourism Brings Gifts and Woes

オーバーツーリズム、サンタの故郷でも

AFP-JIJI

Key Expressions 1

CD2-22

音声を聞いて１～３の（　）内に適当な語を書き入れましょう。

1. In short, overtourism occurs when too many tourists visit a particular (d _ _ _ _ _ _ _ _ _ _ _).
   手短かに言えば、あまりにも多くの観光客がある特定の目的地を訪れるとオーバーツーリズムが起こる。

2. Since the 1980s, tourism chiefs have set out to market the main town, Rovaniemi, as the world's (o _ _ _ _ _ _ _) home of Santa Claus.
   1980 年代以降、観光業界のトップたちは（ラップランドの）中心都市ロヴァニエミを世界公認のサンタクロースの故郷として売り出すことにした。

3. The (r _ _ _ _ _ _ _) council laid out a four-year plan for making tourism more environmentally and socially friendly.
   地方議会は、観光産業を環境的・社会的により優しくするための４年計画を明らかにした。

● Key Expressions 2

over- は「上に、過度に、～を超えて」などの意味をもつ接頭辞です。反対に、under- は「下に、不十分に」などの意味を表します。

枠内の接頭辞の説明と日本語訳を参考に、以下の１～５の動詞にいずれかの接頭辞をプラスした動詞を書き入れましょう。

1. come → [ ]（乗り越える、克服する）
2. crowd → [ ]（混雑する、過密になる）
3. estimate → [ ]（過小評価する）
4. lie → [ ]（根底にある、裏に潜む）
5. take → [ ]（追い越す、～にまさる）

● Key Expressions 3

英語では「多くの～」を意味する表現が大変多く、可算名詞か不可算名詞かの区別だけでなく、生き物の群れの場合はその種類によって異なる表現が用いられます。日本語訳を参考に、以下の１～４の英文の（　　）内に入る適切な語句を選択肢から選び、書き入れましょう。

1. Local media regularly carry stories of ( ) visitors causing disturbances in town.
地元メディアは町で騒ぎを起こす大勢の観光客のニュースを定期的に報じる。

2. The photographer used a drone to film the migration of a ( ) reindeer across Norway to Finland.
その写真家はドローンを使い、トナカイの巨大な群れのノルウェーからフィンランドへの移動を撮影した。

3. Finland is Europe's most heavily-forested country. Land with trees can hold ( ) water that would otherwise stream down hills and surge into towns.
フィンランドはヨーロッパでもっとも森林の多い国である。木々のある土地は、木がなければ丘を流れ下り、町まで押し寄せるであろう大量の水を蓄えることが可能である。

4. A ( ) geese gather at Lake Saimaa in Finland in summer.
ガンの大きな群れが、夏にフィンランドのサイマー湖に集まる。

massive herd of	large flock of	hordes of	vast amounts of

● Background Knowledge

北欧の少数民族サーミ人について、英文に述べられているものを1～4から選びましょう。

Finland's remote Lapland region is the homeland of the indigenous Sami people, who protest that some in the tourist industry spread offensive stereotypes about Sami people and seek to profit from their ancient culture. "Almost every day there are people coming to the Sami area asking 'Where can I see the shamans, where are the Sami witches?' " the president of Finland's Sami Parliament said. "It's only a picture that the tourism industry has created and developed." Last year, the Sami Parliament issued guidelines for "ethically responsible" behavior from tour operators and visitors in order to preserve Sami culture.

The Japan Times (AFP-JIJI)

Notes indigenous「先住民の」 shaman「シャーマン」

1. サーミ人は観光産業を主な収入源として、昔から多くの観光客をもてなしてきた。
2. フィンランドの観光事業者は、サーミ人の抗議を不当として反論している。
3. シャーマンや魔女を探して、サーミ人の暮らす地域にやってくる観光客は稀である。
4. サーミ議会はサーミ文化を守るために観光に関するガイドラインを発表した。

● Newspaper English

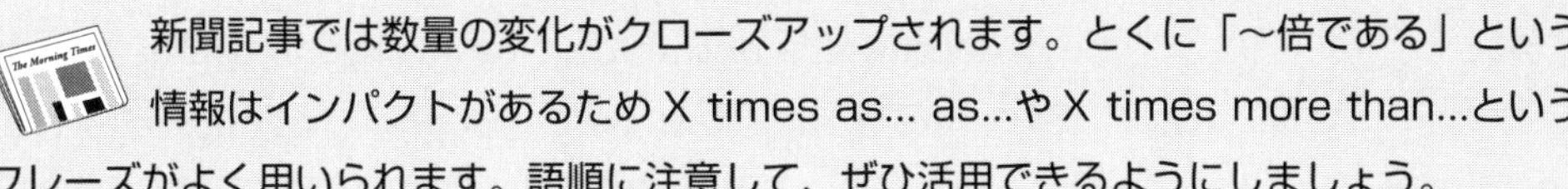

新聞記事では数量の変化がクローズアップされます。とくに「～倍である」という情報はインパクトがあるため X times as... as...や X times more than...というフレーズがよく用いられます。語順に注意して、ぜひ活用できるようにしましょう。

日本語訳を参考に、以下の1と2の英文の［　　］内の語句を正しく並べ替えましょう。

1. The Lapland region, scientists say, is heating up [fast / as / as / the global average / twice].
ラップランド地方は世界平均の2倍の速さで気温が上昇している、と科学者たちは言う。

____

2. Some 45,000 Chinese tourists visited Lapland in 2018— [more / in 2015 / four times / than].
2018年にはおよそ45,000人もの中国人観光客がラップランドを訪れたが、それは2015年の4倍以上であった。

____

● Reading

woe「苦悩」
Statistics Finland「フィンランド統計局」
booming「成長著しい」
specter「(将来への) 悪影響」
mass tourism「マスツーリズム（観光の大衆化、大量の観光客が発生すること)」
tranquility「静けさ」
soil...「〜を汚す」
pristine wilderness「手つかずの原野」
recurring grievance「繰り返えされる苦情の原因」
rental「賃貸物件」
mess「混乱」
dog-sledding entrepreneur「犬ぞり事業主」
major player「大手事業主」
all but...「ほとんど〜」
green credentials「緑化認証」
emissions-heavy「(二酸化炭素) 排出量の多い」
offset...「〜を埋め合わせる」
responsible tourism「レスポンシブル・ツーリズム（責任あ

In the Lapland home of Santa Claus tourism brings gifts and woes

Every year this decade, the visitor figures to Lapland have reached new highs, hitting 2.9 million overnight stays last year, up from 2.2 million in 2010, according to Statistics Finland.

Booming tourism helped drive Rovaniemi's unemployment rate down to below 10 percent last December, its lowest since 1990. However, the specter of mass tourism is a growing concern in a region where residents have traditionally valued tranquility and closeness to nature above all else.

Local media regularly carry stories of tourists soiling the pristine wilderness with rubbish and empty beer cans, or of hordes of visitors causing disturbances in town. Also a recurring grievance is the popularity of accommodation-sharing site Airbnb, says Satu Loiro, Lapland Regional Council's senior tourism advisor. Locals blame the rentals for noise, overcrowding and mess, as well as pushing up housing costs.

The concerns are not shared by everyone, though. "I hope that this individual tourism, people staying in Airbnbs, people traveling individually, will grow," dog-sledding entrepreneur Valentijn Beets said. "They're actually spreading the money straight to the people without any major players in between." His voice all but drowned out by the howls of 120 huskies, Beets added that his clients care about animal welfare and green credentials.

Lapland's remoteness and the long distances make for emissions-heavy travel in the region, which scientists say is heating up twice as fast as the global average. The council plans to encourage tourists to pay to offset their air-travel carbon emissions as well as develop better rail and public transport links. Loiro said there was now a "responsible tourism network" of operators who recently published a list of "100 deeds for sustainable tourism."

"This includes respecting the Sami culture or using local food, and using biofuels," Loiro said. The regional council recently laid out a four-year plan for making tourism more environmentally and socially friendly while still encouraging it to grow, she added.

〈参考〉Airbnb「エアビーアンドビー」: 世界各国の現地の人たちが、自宅などを宿泊施設として提供するネット上のマッチングサービス。

The Japan Times (AFP-JIJI)

る観光)」
sustainable tourism「サステイナブル・ツーリズム（持続可能な観光)」
biofuel「バイオ燃料」

Summary

CD2-25

以下の空所１～４に当てはまる語を選択肢から選び、書き入れましょう。

The Finnish region of Lapland has enjoyed year-on-year (1.   ) in the number of tourists visiting the area, boosting the local economy and reducing (2.   ). However, the increase in tourist numbers has also led to increases in (3.   ), social disturbances, housing costs and fuel emissions. Efforts to avoid the effects of (4.   ) include a "responsible tourism" business network and a regional council plan to ensure future growth is environmentally and socially responsible.

growth	overtourism	litter	unemployment

● Comprehension 1

ヴァレンタイン・ビーツさんについて、本文の内容に当てはまるものには T（True）を、当てはまらないものには F（False）を（　　）内に書き入れましょう。

1. He runs a dog-sledding business in Lapland. (　　)

2. He sees potential in individual tourists who are staying in Airbnb rentals. (　　)

3. There are at least 120 kennels for his huskies. (　　)

4. His clients are not concerned about animal welfare or the natural environment. (　　)

● Comprehension 2

本文の内容に合うように、1と2の英文を完成させるのに適当なものを、3の質問の答えとして適当なものを、a～dから選びましょう。

1. According to the article,

a. the number of regional visitors jumped by 700,000 overnight.
b. unemployment in one town had decreased since 1990, but is now rising.
c. the yearly number of overnight stays has increased annually over ten years.
d. tourists now make up just under ten percent of Rovaniemi's population.

2. Some locals claim that the popularity of Airbnb rentals has led to

a. strict laws prohibiting public noise.
b. higher prices in the local housing market.
c. violent incidents involving crowds.
d. pressure on the region's waste disposal infrastructure.

3. Which of the following is NOT mentioned as one of the "100 deeds for sustainable tourism"?

a. Respecting indigenous ways of life
b. Consuming local food
c. Restricting the number of incoming flights
d. Using fuel derived from biomass

Chapter 17

Cloning Your Pets

今一度きみに会いたい

AFP-JIJI

● Key Expressions 1

CD2-26

音声を聞いて1～3の（　　）内に適当な語を書き入れましょう。

1. China's first cloned kitten, Garlic, is (s _ _ _ _) Monday at the pet-cloning company Sinogene in Beijing.
   北京にあるペットのクローン作製会社シノジーン社において、月曜日に、中国初のクローン子猫「ニンニク（大蒜）」が姿を現した。

2. According to the owner, the new Garlic is (s _ _ _ _ _ _) to his old white-and-gray cat in appearance.
   飼い主によると、新しいニンニクは、外見が彼の以前飼っていた白と灰色の体毛の猫に似ている。

3. He says the (s _ _ _ _ _ _ _ _ _) between the two cats is more than 90 percent.
   彼によると、2匹の猫の類似度は90パーセントを超えるという。

● Key Expressions 2

同様の意味を持った熟語の場合、伴われる前置詞が同じになることが多いです。まとめて覚えておくようにしましょう。

以下の１～４の動詞句について、伴われる前置詞を（　　）内に書き入れましょう。

1. ～のことで誰かを責める
[blame / criticize] someone (　　　　　　　　　　)...

2. A を B とみなす
[regard / see / view / think of / look on] A (　　　　　　　　　　) B

3. ～の埋め合わせをする
[compensate / make up] (　　　　　　　　　　)...

4. ～に頼る
[depend / rely] (　　　　　　　　　　)...

● Key Expressions 3

動詞の現在分詞と過去分詞が形容詞の働きをする場合、修飾する名詞との関係で形が決まります。動詞と修飾される名詞が能動の関係（～している）なら現在分詞、受け身の関係（～される）なら過去分詞を用いて名詞を修飾します。

以下の１～３の（　　）内の動詞を適当な分詞に変化させましょう。

1. Garlic is a (clone → 　　　　　　　　　　) cat.
ニンニクはクローン猫である。

2. With a (grow → 　　　　　　　　　　) pet market in China, the market for pet cloning is also set to rocket.
中国のペット市場の成長により、ペットクローン化の市場も急成長しようとしている。

3. Animals (create → 　　　　　　　　　　) using cloning technology do not necessarily die prematurely.
クローン技術を使って作製された動物は、必ずしも早死にするわけではない。

● Background Knowledge

ペットのクローン化について、英文に述べられているものを１～４から選びましょう。

Pet cloning is illegal in many countries, but approved in some, including South Korea and the U.S., where singer Barbra Streisand announced last year she had cloned her dog.

The first major success in animal cloning was Dolly the sheep, born in Britain in 1996 as the first mammal cloned from an adult cell. In 2005, researchers in South Korea cloned the first dog. The Sooam Biotech Research Foundation in Seoul says it has cloned some 800 pets and charges $100,000 each.

The Japan Times (AFP-JIJI)

1. ペットのクローン化が法律で許可されている国はない。
2. アメリカの歌手バーブラ・ストライサンドは飼い猫をクローン化した。
3. 羊のドリーは、はじめて受精卵から作製されたクローンである。
4. 初めて犬のクローンを作製した国は韓国である。

● Newspaper English

ニュース記事では、主張や結論に結びつかないような事例や条件を強調するために、「～だけれども」という表現が頻出します。

以下の１と２の（　　）内に当てはまる語を選択肢から選び、書き入れましょう。なお、文頭に来る語も小文字で与えられています。

1. (　　　　　　　　) the high price tag, not all clients were high earners.
高値にもかかわらず、すべての顧客が高額所得者というわけではなかった。

2. (　　　　　　　　) adult pandas are large in size, baby pandas are smaller than kittens.
= Adult pandas are large in size, (　　　　　　　　) baby pandas are smaller than kittens.
大人のパンダはサイズが大きいが、赤ちゃんパンダは子猫よりも小さい。

but	despite	though

Reading

Copycat: Chinese firm creates the first cloned kitten

BEIJING—Seven months after Huang Yu's pet cat Garlic died, the British shorthair was given a 10th life.

Born on July 21, the new Garlic was created by the Chinese firm Sinogene, becoming the Beijing-based company's first successfully copied cat.

The pet-cloning outfit has made more than 40 pet dogs—a procedure that costs a hefty 380,000 yuan ($53,000), while the price for a cat comes in at 250,000 yuan ($35,000).

Mi Jidong, the company's chief executive officer, told AFP that despite the high price tag, not all clients were high earners.

"In fact, a large proportion of customers are young people who have only graduated from university in the last few years," he said.

"Whatever the origin of pets, owners will see them as part of the family. Pet cloning meets the emotional needs of young generations."

Huang, 23, was overjoyed on first seeing Garlic's second incarnation, saying the "similarity between the two cats is more than 90 percent."

"When Garlic died, I was very sad," said Huang. "I couldn't face the facts because it was a sudden death. I blame myself for not taking him to the hospital in time, which led to his death."

The happy owner says he hopes the personality of the new Garlic is as similar to his old white-and-gray cat as its appearance.

With a growing pet market in China, and a huge appetite among their owners for spending, Mi thinks the market for pet cloning is also set to rocket.

According to a report by Pet Fair Asia and pet website *Goumin.com*, pet-related spending in China reached 170.8 billion yuan ($23.7 billion) in 2018. And the country's

copycat「模造品」
outfit「企業」
procedure「作業、手順」
hefty「かなりの」
yuan「元（ユアン）：中国の貨幣単位」
chief executive officer「最高経営責任者」
a large proportion of...「〜の大部分」
emotional「感情面の」
generation「世代」
be overjoyed「大喜びする」
incarnation「肉体の姿」
personality「個性」
appearance「外見」
appetite「意欲」
rocket「急成長する」

scientists have big aspirations for their next cloning challenge, working on the theory that if cats can be cloned, so can pandas.

Chen Dayuan—an expert at the Chinese Academy of Sciences who has been researching giant panda cloning for 20 years—said there could even be scope for cats to give birth to cloned baby pandas, which are smaller than kittens despite their large size when fully grown.

The Japan Times(AFP-JIJI)

have an aspiration for...「～に期待する」
work on...「～に取り組む」
theory「仮説、理論」
scope「機会」
give birth to...「～を産む」

Summary

CD2-29

以下の空所１～４に当てはまる語を選択肢から選び、書き入れましょう。

A Chinese company has successfully cloned a pet cat for the first time, reflecting a (1.) market for pet cloning. Despite the (2.) costs, customers are willing to pay in the hope of reestablishing the important (3.) bond they shared with pets that often felt like family members. In the future, experts in China believe that the technology could even be used to clone (4.) pandas.

high	giant	emotional	growing

● Comprehension 1

クローン猫のニンニクに対する黄さんの感想について本文に述べられているものを、以下の１～５から２つ選びましょう。

1. He felt as if it had the same character as his old cat.
2. It looked almost identical to his old cat.
3. It made him much happier after being so depressed.
4. He was afraid it might die suddenly.
5. He thought its cloning had cost him a lot of money for very little pay out.

● Comprehension 2

本文の内容に合うように、１と３の英文を完成させるのに適当なものを、２の質問の答えとして適当なものを、a～dから選びましょう。

1. The article suggests that people might be surprised by the
a. fact that cats are more expensive to clone than dogs.
b. difficulty faced by scientists trying to clone cats.
c. large number of pet-cloning companies opening in Beijing.
d. relatively young age of many people paying for the service.

2. Which word best describes Mi Jidong's feeling about the future demand for pet cloning?
a. Hopeful
b. Unrealistic
c. Doubtful
d. Cautious

3. Chen Dayuan is
a. the first person to have successfully cloned a panda.
b. a researcher who has become a critic of commercial pet cloning.
c. a market analyst who specializes in the pet industry.
d. a scientist who has spent two decades working on cloning.

Chapter 18

Old Flowers Come Back to Life

一度使われた花束に新たな輝きを

AFP-JIJI

● Key Expressions 1

CD2-30

音声を聞いて１～３の（　　）内に適当な語を書き入れましょう。

1. People usually (t _ _ _ _) away old bouquets the day after they use them at a big event.
人々は、大きなイベントで使った翌日には古い花束をたいてい捨ててしまう。

2. Repeat Roses, a flower service company, was (f _ _ _ _ _ _ _) so that luxury clients could donate used bouquets more easily.
高級志向の顧客が使用済みの花束をもっと気軽に寄付できるように、リピートローズというフラワーサービス会社が設立された。

3. Recycled flowers are donated to hospitals, (n _ _ _ _ _ _) homes, and family shelters.
再利用された花は、病院や老人ホーム、家族のシェルターに寄付されている。

● Key Expressions 2

一般動詞に接尾辞 -er や -or を付けると「～する人」「～する物、道具」という意味の名詞にすることができます。

以下の 1 ～ 5 の動詞に -er や -or を付けて人や物を表す名詞に書き換えましょう。

1. found（創設する） → [ ]（創設者）
2. act（演技する） → [ ]（俳優）
3. direct（指導する） → [ ]（指導者）
4. govern（統治する） → [ ]（知事）
5. copy（複写する） → [ ]（コピー機）

● Key Expressions 3

go（離れていく）、get（ある状態を手に入れる）、make（作る、ある状態に変える）など、基本動詞と呼ばれる動詞は、別の単語と組み合わさってイディオムとなり、一つの意味を成すことがあります。日常会話の中でもよく使われるため、それぞれの語のイメージを覚えておくと意味の理解に役立ちます。

日本語訳を参考に、以下の 1 ～ 3 の英文の（ ）内に当てはまる基本動詞（go, get, make）を適当な形に変えて書き入れましょう。

1. Regifting often ( ) a bad rap, but it can actually be the most thoughtful gesture.
受け取った贈り物を他の人にあげることはしばしば非難をされるが、実は最も心のこもった行為になり得る。

2. It is disgusting when we think about the amount of resources that ( ) into the flowers.
花に投入される資源の量を考えると嫌な気分になる。

3. A wedding designer founded Repeat Roses to ( ) it easier for luxury clients to donate used bouquets.
ある結婚式のデザイナーは、高級志向の顧客が使用済みの花束をもっと気軽に寄付できるようにリピートローズ社を設立した。

● Background Knowledge

結婚式などで廃棄される花を再利用するある団体について、英文に述べられていないものを１～４から選びましょう。

Random Acts of Flowers, Knoxville, a Tennessee-based nonprofit organization, does not resell blooms but instead helps facilitate the donations. Founded in 2008, the group works with hospitals and nursing homes to brighten patients' days with the leftover flowers, which come from weddings, funerals, and grocery store surplus. In the past 10 years, it has delivered more than 340,000 bouquets and repurposed more than 356,000 vases.

Bloomberg

Notes bloom「花」 facilitate...「～を促進する」 surplus「余ったもの」

1. テネシー州を拠点とする非営利団体である。
2. 結婚式などで残った花を使って、病院や老人ホームの患者の生活を明るくしている。
3. 10 年間で 34 万個以上の花束を病院から寄付してもらった。
4. 花束だけでなく、花瓶も再利用してきた。

● Newspaper English

語句の後ろにダッシュ（—）を続け、その後ろに補足情報や具体例を付け加えることができます。和訳する時は、ダッシュの部分を「つまり」や「すなわち」と置き換えてみましょう。

以下の１～３の文章の後ろに付けるべき適切な補足情報を a ～ c から選びましょう。

1. Jennifer Grove founded Repeat Roses—(　　　).
2. Regifting can be the most thoughtful gesture—(　　　).
3. New services are popping up for eco-conscious customers—(　　　).

a. especially young ones
b. both for the recipient and the environment
c. a New York City-based flower service company

Valentine's Day flowers don't have to be so bad for the Earth after all

Regifting often gets a bad rap, but it can actually be the most thoughtful gesture—both for the recipient and the environment.

As consumers, especially young ones, become more eco-conscious, services are popping up to reduce wastefulness in the flower industry, extending the life of old bouquets that were previously thrown away the day after a big event. Considering that the floral gifting market is expected to reach $16 billion in revenue by 2023, buying from eco-friendly operations can have a huge impact.

According to one estimate, the roughly 100 million roses grown for a typical Valentine's Day in the U.S. produce about 9,000 metric tons of carbon dioxide emissions.

"When you realize what the supply chain looks like and the number of hands that touch these flowers, and then they're only appreciated for a couple of hours, it's kind of disgusting when you think about the amount of resources that go into it," says Jennifer Grove, founder of New York City-based flower service Repeat Roses.

While working as a wedding designer and corporate planner, Grove often oversaw the design of intricate floral arrangements, only to see those creations discarded within a few hours. In 2014, she founded Repeat Roses to make it easier for luxury clients to donate used bouquets. Like a traditional floral service, the company sells high-end floral decorations for weddings or social events, but it then recycles or composts them.

If a customer chooses the signature repurposing service, a Repeat Roses team can remove the arrangements from the event and then restyle the flowers into petite bouquets to donate to hospitals, nursing homes, and family shelters. If there's a charity that holds a special place in a customer's

wastefulness「浪費」
revenue「収益」
operation「事業者」
metric ton「メートルトン」
carbon dioxide「二酸化炭素」
appreciate...「〜を大切にする」
oversee...「〜を監督する」
intricate「複雑な」
only to...「〜する結果となる」
discard...「〜を処分する」
high-end「高級志向の」
compost...「〜を堆肥にする」
signature「代表的な」
petite「小ぶりの、小さい」
charity「慈善団体」

heart, the team will ensure the blooms are sent there. Examples include the American Cancer Society's Hope Lodge at the Jerome L. Greene Family Center and the Bowery Mission Women's Center in Manhattan.

"It's a logistics business, and we're trying to make sure we are strategic in where we play matchmaker," Grove says. When the charities are finished with the flowers, Repeat Roses also picks them back up and composts them.

logistics「物流」
strategic「戦略的な」
matchmaker「仲介人」

Bloomberg

● Summary

以下の空所１～４に当てはまる語を選択肢から選び、書き入れましょう。

Despite the flower industry's reputation for (1.), a New York-based luxury florist has found a way to make its business (2.) more environmentally friendly and socially conscious. It does so by first donating flowers that are no longer needed by a (3.), and then composting those flower arrangements once they are past their prime. When they place their order, the original clients can even choose which (4.) the flowers get given to.

organization	wastefulness	client	model

● Comprehension 1

以下の１～４の出来事を、時系列に並べ替えましょう。

1. Repeat Roses picks up the old flowers and composts them.
2. The old flowers are remade into small bouquets and donated to the hospital.
3. Jennifer Grove founded a flower service company, Repeat Roses.
4. A customer chooses the signature repurposing service.

(　　　) → (　　　) → (　　　) → (　　　)

● Comprehension 2

本文の内容に合うように、１と２の英文を完成させるのに適当なものを、３の質問の答えとして適当なものを、a～d から選びましょう。

1. The article suggests that the market for floral gifts is expected to
   a. grow over the next few years.
   b. shrink due to changing consumer tastes.
   c. be extended by new environmental regulations.
   d. suffer from the impact of scandals.

2. Jennifer Grove believes that
   a. the government should exert more control over the supply chain.
   b. it is shameful to use flowers for only a very short time.
   c. people can make their flowers last longer by not touching them.
   d. the pressure to spend money on Valentine's Day is disgusting.

3. Which of the following services does Repeat Roses NOT provide?
   a. A disposal service for old flower arrangements
   b. A dating service for single New Yorkers
   c. A delivery service for rearranged flowers
   d. A decoration service for wedding ceremonies

Chapter 19

No Snow? Let's Make Some!

夏だって、スキーに夢中

AFP-JIJI

● Key Expressions 1

CD2-34

音声を聞いて１～３の（　　）内に適当な語を書き入れましょう。

1. Mountains, snow and winter sports are (s _ _ _ _ _ _ _) of Norway.
山、雪、そしてウィンタースポーツは、ノルウェーの象徴である。

2. Norwegians would like to (e _ _ _ _) skiing during the summer too.
ノルウェー人は夏もスキーを楽しみたいと思っている。

3. There is a market for (f _ _ _ _ _ _ _ _ _) where people can ski during the warmer months.
人々が暖かい時期にスキーができる施設には需要がある。

● Key Expressions 2

以下の１～４はウィンタースポーツに関する語句です。日本語の意味に合うように、適当なものを選択肢から選び、(　　) 内に書き入れましょう。

1. (　　　　　　　　　　) the run　［斜面を滑り降りる］
2. (　　　　　　　　　　) on the ramps　［スロープでジャンプの練習をする］
3. (　　　　　　　　　　) on picnic chairs ［ピクニックチェアで休む］
4. (　　　　　　　　　　) a taste of ski experience during summer
［夏場にスキー体験を味わいたい］

rest	want	practice jumps	glide down

● Key Expressions 3

群前置詞とは、２つ以上の語が合わさって１つの前置詞の働きをするものです。これらは長文の中でもよく出てくるので、フレーズで覚えておくと便利です。

日本語訳を参考に、以下の１～３の (　　) 内に入る適当な群前置詞を選択肢から選び、書き入れましょう。なお、文頭に来る語も小文字で与えられています。

1. (　　　　　　　　　　) the U.S. National Oceanic and Atmospheric Administration, last month was the hottest January in 141 years.
米国海洋大気庁によると、先月は、141 年間の中で最も暑い１月となった。

2. SNØ Resort was opened in Norway (　　　　　　　　　　) tourists who might want a taste of the Scandinavian ski experience during the summer.
スノ・リゾートは、夏の間にスカンジナビアのスキー体験を味わいたいかもしれない観光客のために、ノルウェーで開業した。

3. (　　　　　　　　　　) climate change, the lack of snow has impacted the tourism industry from the Alps in France, Switzerland and Austria to the Chilean Andes.
気候の変化に伴い、雪不足はフランス、スイス、オーストリアのアルプスからチリのアンデスまでの観光産業に影響を与えている。

for the sake of	along with	according to

● Background Knowledge

ノルウェーの屋内スキー場スノ・リゾートについて、英文に述べられていないものを１～４から選びましょう。

In early February this year, just outside SNØ Resort, the thick Scandinavian forests were a lush green and a nearby lake was unfrozen. A floating platform for swimmers and sunbathers in summer was still in place, and thermometers marked some 5 degrees Celsius, compared to the usual sub-zero temperatures.

SNØ Resort sits on a mountain slope just 15 kilometers (9.3 miles) away from the capital Oslo and can host 350,000 skiers a year, with adults paying 350 kroner ($38) for a day pass. It features a 500-meter slope for downhill and 1-kilometer to 1.5-kilometer cross country track.

Bloomberg

Notes sub-zero「氷点下の」 kroner「クローネ（ノルウェーの通貨）」

1. 2月上旬、スノ・リゾートのすぐ外では湖が凍っていた。
2. スノ・リゾートの周辺では、2月時点でも水泳ができるよう整備されていた。
3. スノ・リゾートは、首都オスロからわずか 15 キロ（9.3 マイル）離れた山の斜面にある。
4. スノ・リゾートの下り坂には、500 メートルのスロープがある。

● Newspaper English

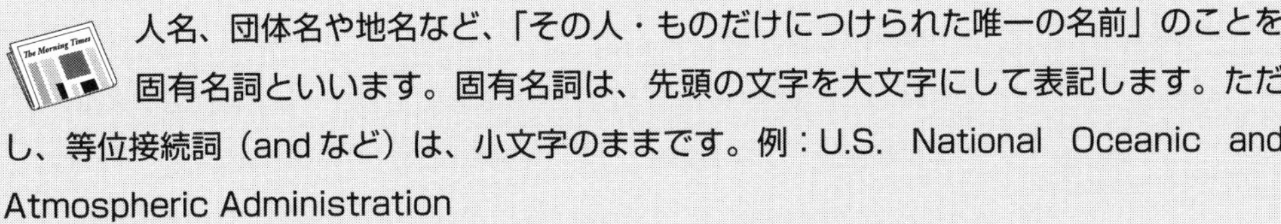

人名、団体名や地名など、「その人・ものだけにつけられた唯一の名前」のことを固有名詞といいます。固有名詞は、先頭の文字を大文字にして表記します。ただし、等位接続詞（and など）は、小文字のままです。例：U.S. National Oceanic and Atmospheric Administration

以下の１と２の文には固有名詞が含まれています。固有名詞の箇所に下線を引きましょう。

1. Europe's Copernicus Climate Change Service reported that some areas in northeastern Europe were more than 6 degrees above the 1981–2010 January average.
ヨーロッパのコペルニクス気候変動サービスは、ヨーロッパ北東部の一部の地域で 1981 年から 2010 年の１月の平均気温より６度以上、上回ったと報告した。

2. The project is the brainchild of Olav Selvaag.
そのプロジェクトは、オラフ・セルヴァーグ氏の発案である。

Reading

Now even Norwegians are skiing indoors in winter

On a Monday morning in February, skiers glided down the run, while snowboarders nearby practiced jumps on the ramps and tired visitors rested on red picnic chairs and munched snacks as they recovered.

The scene could be that of any winter morning at any ski resort in Norway—the cradle of modern skiing—except that snow hadn't fallen from the sky, and the view of a powder-coated Scandinavian forest was printed on a giant panel built on the side of the slope.

Norway's SNØ Resort opened its doors just one month ago, during the country's warmest January on record. The project is the brainchild of Olav Selvaag, a member of one of Norway's richest families, known for real estate and property development. Among the owners is Norwegian billionaire Stein Erik Hagen.

Selvaag conceived the installation for locals to use during winter when bad weather hits the real resorts, and for ski addicts and tourists who might want a taste of the Scandinavian ski experience during the summer. Now, climate change and unusually warm winter weather have altered that plan.

"The winters are varying a bit more than one could wish," said SNØ Managing Director Morten Dybdahl. "They have become shorter and there's more variation, therefore, there's an even greater market for a facility like this."

Last month was the hottest January in the 141 years that global temperature records have been kept, according to the U.S. National Oceanic and Atmospheric Administration. Europe's Copernicus Climate Change Service reported that some areas in northeastern Europe were more than 6 degrees above the 1981–2010 January average. Some parts of Norway were 25 degrees Celsius warmer than usual.

On the ground, that has resulted in one of the worst ski

munch...「～を（むしゃむしゃ）食べる」
cradle「発祥の地」
open its door「開業する」
on record「記録された」
conceive...「～を考案する」
installation「施設」
addict「愛好家」
alter...「～を変える」
Celsius「摂氏」

seasons ever in Norway, a country where the sport has become a key part of the culture and of people's identity. This year Norwegians are not alone in lamenting the weather—climate change and the lack of snow has impacted the tourism industry from the Alps in France, Switzerland and Austria to the Chilean Andes.

Bloomberg

lament... 「～を嘆く」

● Summary

以下の空所１～４に当てはまる語を選択肢から選び、書き入れましょう。

Despite being (1.   ) and economically important to many Norwegians, skiing—even in winter—is under threat due to the effects of climate change. After the hottest January since global temperature record-keeping began, Norway (2.   ) experienced one of its worst ever ski seasons. A (3.   ) built indoor ski facility, (4.   ) intended to cater to skiers during summer and extreme winter conditions, is anticipated to be popular all year around.

culturally	unfortunately	originally	newly

● Comprehension 1

以下の１～４は文脈によって色々な意味を持つ単語です。本文中で使われている意味をａ～ｄから選びましょう。

1. climate ( )
2. facility ( )
3. identity ( )
4. interest ( )

a. place designed to fulfill a particular function
b. the typical weather conditions in a particular area
c. a feeling of special attention toward something
d. the distinguishing aspects or qualities of a person or group of people

● Comprehension 2

本文の内容に合うように、１と３の英文を完成させるのに適当なものを、２の質問の答えとして適当なものを、ａ～ｄから選びましょう。

1. In p.122 line 6, Norway is referred to as "the cradle of modern skiing." This suggests that Norway
a. has the highest number of ski slopes among modern countries.
b. has consistently been rated the best place to ski in the world.
c. is widely thought of as the easiest place for young children to learn to ski.
d. is considered to be the place where the modern sport developed.

2. Who had the original idea for the SNØ Resort?
a. Olav Selvaag
b. The minister for real estate and property development
c. Stein Erik Hagen
d. Morten Dybdahl

3. The article suggests that
a. climate change threatens a core component of the Norwegian identity.
b. European skiers are already changing their focus to South America.
c. the energy consumed by indoor ski slopes also contributes to climate change.
d. the facility could be even more popular in other countries.

Chapter 20

Promising iPS Cell Technology

進歩するiPS細胞移植

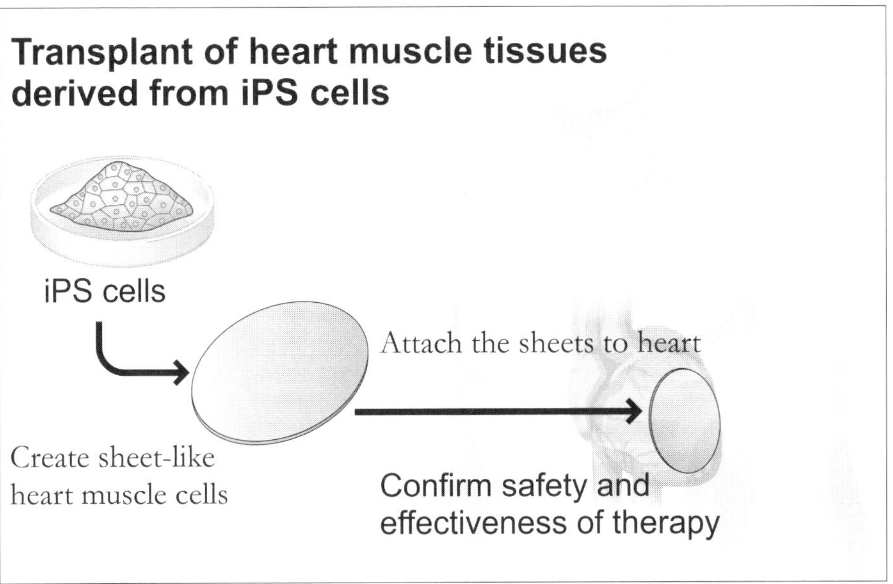

The Asahi Shimbun

● Key Expressions 1

CD2-38

音声を聞いて１～３の（　　）内に適当な語を書き入れましょう。

1. An Osaka University team successfully conducted the world's first (t __________) of cardiac muscle cells using induced pluripotent stem cells, or iPS cells.
大阪大学のあるチームが人工多能性幹細胞、すなわち iPS 細胞を使って、世界初の心筋細胞移植に成功した。

2. Three sheets of heart muscle tissue made from iPS cells were attached to (a _______) parts of the patient's heart.
iPS 細胞から作られた心筋組織のシート 3 枚が、患者の心臓の患部に貼り付けられた。

3. The sheets are 4 to 5 centimeters in (d ________) and 0.1 millimeter thick.
そのシートは直径 4 ～ 5 センチメートル、厚さ 0.1 ミリメートルである。

● Key Expressions 2

接頭辞 cardio-, cardi- は「心臓」という意味を持ち、様々な語とくっついて色々な語句を形成します。

日本語訳を参考に、以下の１～５の（　　）内に適当な語を選択肢より選び、書き入れましょう。複数回使うものもあります。

1. (　　　　　　　　) muscle cells　　心筋細胞
2. ischemic (　　　　　　　　)　　虚血性心筋症
3. (　　　　　　　　) surgery　　心臓血管手術
4. (　　　　　　　　) blood vessels　　心臓の血管
5. (　　　　　　　　)　　心臓病学

cardiovascular	cardiology	cardiac	cardiomyopathy

● Key Expressions 3

日本語訳を参考に、以下の１～３の英文の［　　］内の語句を正しい語順に並べかえましょう。

1. The clinical trial of the transplant was postponed [a powerful earthquake / due / damage / from / to] that hit Osaka Prefecture and rendered the cell cultivation facility unusable.
大阪を襲い、細胞を培養する施設を使用できなくした大きな地震による損害のせいで、（iPS 細胞）移植の臨床試験は延期された。

____

2. Hideyuki Okano, professor of molecular neurobiology at Keio University, is researching the application of iPS-derived nerve cells to [damage / with / treat / spinal cord / patients] .
慶應義塾大学の分子神経生物学教授、岡野栄之氏は、脊髄を損傷した患者を治療するため、iPS 由来の神経細胞の応用を研究している。

____

3. The iPS cells were created [tissue / from / by / a healthy donor / provided] .
その iPS 細胞は健康なドナーによって提供された組織から作られた。

____

● Background Knowledge

iPS細胞を使った移植について、英文に述べられていないものを1～4から選びましょう。

The world's first transplant of iPS-derived cells was conducted in 2014 when the Riken research institute transplanted retinal cells for a patient with age-related macular degeneration. In 2018, Kyoto University transplanted nerve cells for a Parkinson disease patient. Osaka University transplanted cornea cells into a patient with a disease of the cornea in 2019. Patients who undergo transplants using iPS-derived cells must accept the risk that the cells may become cancerous. The more iPS-derived cells a patient receives, the higher the risk.

Hundreds of thousands of retina cells were used in the 2014 retina transplant. In the 2018 and 2019 transplants, the number of nerve and cornea cells used soared to between 5 million and 6 million.

The Asahi Shimbun

Notes retinal「網膜の」 cornea「角膜」

1. iPSから作った細胞の世界初の移植は、加齢黄斑変性の患者に対してなされた。
2. 京都大学と大阪大学はともにiPSから作った神経細胞の移植を行った。
3. iPS細胞を使った移植は、細胞が癌化する恐れがある。
4. 2018年と2019年には、使用される神経と角膜のiPS細胞の数は、500～600万に増加した。

● Newspaper English

新聞では、記事の中にトピックに関する過去の情報が盛り込まれ、現在完了や過去完了形で述べられることがあります。

次の1と2の文章の（　　）内に入る適当な動詞を選択肢より選び、適当な形にして書き入れましょう。

1. The Osaka University team (　　　　　　　　　　) to conduct the clinical trial of the transplant earlier, after the government approved the plan in May 2018.
   この大阪大学のチームは、2018年の5月に政府が計画を認可した後、早い時期にこの移植の臨床試験を行う予定にしていた。

2. The patient (　　　　　　　　　　) to a general hospital ward.
   その患者は（今では）一般病棟に移されている。

move	plan

Patient in Japan first to have iPS cell heart muscle transplant

A patient who received the world's first transplant of cardiac muscle cells using artificially derived stem cells known as iPS (induced pluripotent stem) cells this month is in a stable condition, an Osaka University team said Jan. 27.

After surgery, doctors closely monitored the patient, who had ischemic cardiomyopathy, a condition in which clotted arteries cause heart muscles to malfunction. But the patient has been moved to a general hospital ward, the team said.

condition「病気」
clotted artery「動脈の梗塞」
malfunction「機能不全」

Yoshiki Sawa, a professor of cardiovascular surgery at the university, who led the team that conducted the transplant, said the team aims to put the technique into practical use.

Sawa said the team hopes transplants of heart muscle tissue derived from iPS cells "will be used to save many patients who have heart conditions."

In the clinical trial, three sheets of heart muscle tissue made from iPS cells stocked at Kyoto University's Center for iPS Cell Research and Application were attached to affected parts of the patient's heart. The iPS cells were created from tissue provided by a healthy donor.

Kyoto University's Center for iPS Cell Research and Application「京都大学 iPS 細胞研究所」

The sheets were 4 to 5 centimeters in diameter and 0.1 millimeter thick.

The transplant's goal is to regenerate cardiac blood vessels using a substance secreted by the sheets of muscle cells. The sheets are degradable and disappear from the body several months after they secrete the substance, according to the team.

regenerate...「～を再生する」
secrete...「～を分泌する」
degradable「分解できる」

The university plans to perform similar transplants on nine other patients who have serious heart problems.

The Osaka University team had planned to conduct the clinical trial of the transplant earlier, after the government approved the plan in May 2018, but it was postponed due to damage from a powerful earthquake that hit Osaka

Prefecture the following month and rendered its cell cultivation facility unusable.

The trial is part of the process toward the future distribution of medical products using cells.

Osaka University's announcement of the successful transplant of tissue created from iPS cells marked the fourth such transplant.

Including Osaka University's trial, Japanese surgeons have now successfully transplanted tissue created from iPS cells four times.

The Asahi Shimbun

Summary

CD2-41

以下の空所１～４に当てはまる語を選択肢から選び、書き入れましょう。ただし、文頭に来る語も小文字で与えられています。

(1.) in Japan have successfully carried out a transplant of tissue created from induced pluripotent stem (2.), or iPS cells, in a patient who was suffering from heart disease. The patient is recovering well and doctors hope to use the same treatment on other (3.) living with similar heart (4.).

doctors	patients	conditions	cells

● Comprehension 1

本文の内容に合うように、以下の表の１～６の（　　）を埋めましょう。

移植された患者の病気	(1.　　　　　　　　　　)
移植の目的	筋肉細胞のシートによって分泌される (2.　　　　　　　　　　)を使って、 (3.　　　　　　　　　　)を (4.　　　　　　　　　　)すること。
移植された心筋シートの仕様	直径 (5.　　　　　　　　　　)
	厚さ (6.　　　　　　　　　　)

● Comprehension 2

本文の内容に合うように、１と３の質問の答えとして適当なものを、２の英文を完成させるのに適当なものを、a～d から選びましょう。

1. Which of the following techniques did the medical team use?

a. ischemic cardiomyopathy
b. artery clotting
c. tissue transplant
d. artificial monitoring

2. Yoshiki Sawa hopes that

a. the costs involved in such new treatments will now come down.
b. the technique could be used to prevent heart conditions from developing.
c. the number of stem cell donors will continue to increase.
d. the treatment will be offered to more patients in the future.

3. Why was the trial delayed?

a. The government refused to give permission.
b. There was a natural disaster.
c. Four patients died in earlier attempts.
d. Distributing the products was too costly.

Acknowledgements
All the news materials are reprinted by permission of
AFP-JIJI, Bloomberg, The Asahi Shimbun, The Associated Press, The Japan News, The Japan Times and The Washington Post.

TEXT CREDITS

Chapter 1　Accepting Diversity
Saitama beauty salon allows Muslims to let their hair down
The Asahi Shimbun Asia & Japan Watch, September 18, 2019 (partially modified)

Chapter 2　Washi Helps Us Get Through Summer
Paper shoes? Moisture-killer washi taking brave new forms
The Asahi Shimbun Asia & Japan Watch, September 6, 2019 (partially modified)

Chapter 3　The Secrets of the Ocean Floor
Scientists dive into 'Midnight Zone' to study dark ocean
The Associated Press, February 6, 2020 (partially modified)

Chapter 4　What Messages Resonate with You?
Comeback of temple bulletin boards
The Japan News, February 10, 2020 (partially modified)

Chapter 5　Let's Change the World from #KuToo
In Japan, a campaign against high heels targets conformity and discrimination
From The Washington Post. ©2020 The Washington Post. All rights reserved.

Chapter 6　Spiders Will Change the Fashion Industry
Dream fiber that is stronger than steel: synthetic spider silk
The Asahi Shimbun Asia & Japan Watch, November 20, 2019 (partially modified)

Chapter 7　Sharp Decline in Butterfly Population
Nationwide survey finds rapid drop in butterfly population
The Japan News, December 12, 2019 (partially modified)

Chapter 8　Volcanic Ash Attracts Tourists
Sakurajima volcanic ash transformed into art
The Japan News, February 8, 2020 (partially modified)

Chapter 9　Seeking Work-Life Balance
Asics employee's lawsuit highlights paternity leave in Japan
The Associated Press, September 9, 2019 (partially modified)

Chapter 10　For the Empowerment of Women
Tokyo shop deals in embroidery to empower women in Bangladesh
The Asahi Shimbun Asia & Japan Watch, January 28, 2020 (partially modified)

Chapter 11　Setting up Lanes for Self-Driving Cars

Lanes for self-driving vehicles eyed

The Japan News, September 6, 2019 (partially modified)

Chapter 12　High School Hawker Scaring Away Nuisance Birds

Finding success in getting hawks to do what comes naturally to them

The Asahi Shimbun Asia & Japan Watch, January 4, 2020 (partially modified)

Chapter 13　Fusion of AI with Human Sensibility

Movers & Shakers / 'Maverick' designer fuses fashion with science

The Japan News, December 21, 2019 (partially modified)

Chapter 14　Infrastructure Inspection Using Drones

Safety upgrade / Drones, robots to inspect aging bridges, roads

The Japan News, January 26, 2020 (partially modified)

Chapter 15　Use Your Aesthetics in Business

Study art to thrive in business

The Japan News, February 20, 2020 (partially modified)

Chapter 16　Tourism Brings Gifts and Woes

In the Lapland home of Santa Claus–and the Sami people–tourism brings gifts and woes (*AFP-JIJI*)

The Japan Times, December 25, 2019 (partially modified)

Chapter 17　Cloning Your Pets

Copycat: Chinese firm creates the first cloned kitten (*AFP-JIJI*)

The Japan Times, September 5, 2019 (partially modified)

Chapter 18　Old Flowers Come Back to Life

Valentine's Day Flowers Don't Have to Be So Bad for the Earth After All

Bloomberg, January 28, 2020 (partially modified)

Chapter 19　No Snow? Let's Make Some!

Now Even Norwegians Are Skiing Indoors in Winter

Bloomberg, February 15, 2020 (partially modified)

Chapter 20　Promising iPS Cell Technology

Patient in Japan 1st to have iPS cell heart muscle transplant

The Asahi Shimbun Asia & Japan Watch, January 28, 2020 (partially modified)